MILK CANS

THE JOURNEY COMMENCES

"PERFECT MILK CANS are essential to profitable dairying. A milk can is not perfect unless it can be kept absolutely clean and free from germs and unless it will last five or ten years without repairs.

Buhl Stamping Company, Detroit, Michigan.

Sufficient capacity to make every milk can used in the United States".

From a Buhl Stamping Company advertisement in the World Almanac.

◀ *Buhl Stamping Co. 1898 booklet for salesmen.*

MILK CANS

A Celebration of their History, Use, and Design

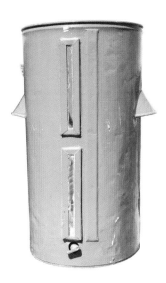

By Ian Spellerberg

Foreword by Marc Allum,
'frequent specialist on the BBC Antiques Road Show'

7351. A Boothea Milkman.

MILK CANS
A Celebration of their History, Use, and Design

Author: Ian Spellerberg
Designer: Anne Schneeberger, Mika Design Ltd.
and Sonya Boushek for Astragal Press
ISBN 978-1-931626-41-5
First published 2018

Northern Hemisphere Edition
Published by Astragal Press
www.astragalpress.com
ISBN: 978-1-931626-41-5

Originally Published by:
Cadsonbury Publications
www.smithsbookshop.co.nz
ISBN: 978-1-1927203-59-0

Also by Ian Spellerberg:

READING & WRITING ACCESSORIES
A Study of Paper-knives, Paper Folders,
Letter Openers and Mythical Page Turners.
2015. Cadsonbury Publications,
New Zealand and Oak Knoll Press, U.S.A.

MATCH HOLDERS
First-hand Accounts of Tinderboxes, Matches, Spills, Vesta Cases.
Match Strikers, and Permanent Matches.
2016. Cadsonbury Publications, New Zealand.

◀ *See P. 145*

CONTENTS

▼ *See P. 141*

FOREWORD BY MARC ALLUM

Professor Ian Spellerberg's request to write a foreword for this book was never going to be a chore. Not only is it highly complimentary that he should think me worthy but it is also rather humbling because one cannot help feeling a little inferior at his innate ability to choose wonderfully thought-provoking subjects that seem to have escaped the usual fields of interest. Indeed, some might be tempted to say that his choice of subject is 'odd' but the truth is actually far from it. One characteristic is immediately apparent; he attacks his chosen theme with an undeniable vigour, which in his own inimitable fashion, means exploring every nook and cranny of the subject, leaving no facet of the topic uninvestigated. Milk Cans is no exception and the almost immediate realisation that the title is little more than a tease, belies the fact that this is an invitation into a world that is much bigger than you could have ever imagined. This is a rigorous and fascinating explanation of a subject that benefits from both the authors academic ability to research his subject judiciously but also his ability to relay it in an approachable and absorbing way.

I've worked in the world of auctions, art and antiques for some thirty years and that breadth of experience has put me into contact with a hugely diverse amount of material. Therefore, armed with some knowledge and first-hand experience of handling objects such as milk cans, churns and dairy related paraphernalia, I was, however - after reading this book – fascinated by what I didn't know. Milk Cans is a highly absorbing historical account of an everyday commodity that we essentially take for granted. Milk and the means to move it and process it, from the most basic of local farmyard scenarios to the bulk movement for huge consumption in cities and by industry, is graphically charted in this work through a wonderful selection of photographs and images sourced from archives and institutions around the world. The remarkably cosmopolitan content ranges in great breadth from the manufacture, advertising, transport, souvenirs, toys and thematic items surrounding the subject but is also given contextual depth by the many issues that still affect modern dairy farmers – such as the politics and social aspects - which have of course always been part and parcel of farming and milk production!

The epilogue is indeed a sombre footnote to the demise of the milk can or churn but the headlines - 'Milk Can Doomed' – were of course inevitable. Professor Spellerberg's book is a remarkably well-researched publication and will no doubt take its place as a definitive work on the subject thus proving a valuable reference aid to both historians and collectors alike!

Marc Allum

PREFACE AND ACKNOWLEDGMENTS

Before the use of milk cans, a common practice was for cows and asses to be driven through the streets. Customers would receive fresh milk directly from the cow. In London, milkmaids avoided the dangers to themselves and contamination of their milk (from slops being thrown out at night from upper storied windows) by shouting "milkmaid below!" or "milko" or even "meow".

A topic of great relevance to milk cans was hygiene and cleanliness. Much has been written about the risks of contaminated milk because, if nothing else, it was sometimes linked to outbreaks of typhoid fever. Pinto, in his book *Treen or Small Woodware through the Ages* (1949) remarked that before the discovery of bacteria, European dairies gave no thought to contamination. Not only has there always been concern about hygienic practices in milk production but there has, for many years, been concern about the cleanliness of empty milk cans. For example in 1916 a formal enquiry was instigated in England concerning the state of cleanliness of empty cans. It showed that up to 2% of rail borne milk was sour on arrival at its destination, with the result that in London alone there was a loss of some 90,000 gallons of milk annually. The many varied designs of milk cans have therefore been in response to the demands for keeping the milk safe from contamination.

Milk can designs are indeed varied. In 1909, Professor E.H. Farrington (Assistant Professor of Dairy Husbandry at the Wisconsin Dairy School) addressed the thirty-fifth annual meeting of the Illinois State Dairymen's Association. He had recently returned from abroad studying milk and milk products. He mentioned how diverse milk cans were overseas compared to those at home and noted "a person interested in making collections could easily find enjoyment in getting together the many different types of milk cans that are used in various countries."

The milk can is the greatest legacy of traditional dairy farming. Not surprising therefore that milk cans have occupied the minds of inventors and engineers. They have inspired artists, toy makers, playwrights, poets, novelty manufacturers, and sports minded people. The image of a milk can has been used widely in advertising from cheese to chocolate. However, it is disappointing to find that there appear to be few collectors of milk cans. There also appears to be is no book on the subject of their use, history and iconic design.

Bulk transport of milk by road and rail may have largely taken over the extensive role of milk cans but that has not brought about the demise of milk cans. Some countries still make and use them. At the same time there is much nostalgia for milk cans, milk can stands and the old methods of transportation.

I could not have written this book without the generous help from many people around the world. My wife (Myfanwy), son (Christopher), and daughter (Kathryn) have often helped locate and obtain many examples of very fine milk cans – as well as accepting what has been my obsession with celebrating milk cans.

My special thanks to my granddaughter Maisie for her help. (See family photograph in the appendices.)

◄ *A three gallon Galvanized tin milk can from the Borden American Dairy. Courtesy History San Jose three gallon Galvanized tin milk can from the Borden American Dairy. Courtesy Histwory San Jose*

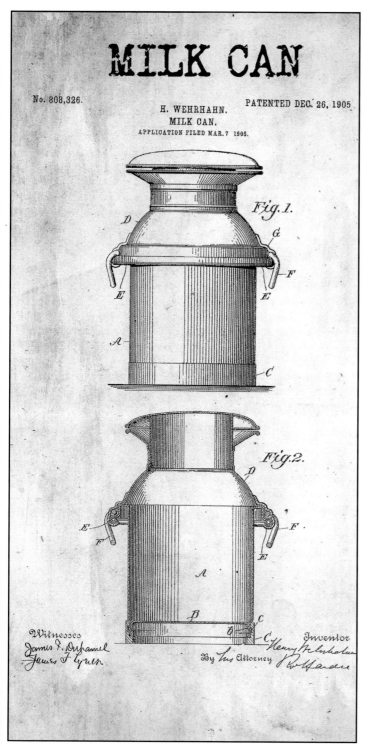

MILK CAN

No. 808,326.

H. WEHRHAHN.
MILK CAN.
APPLICATION FILED MAR. 7 1905.

PATENTED DEC. 26, 1905.

Fig.1.

Fig.2.

Witnesses
James F. Duhamel
James F. Gruen

Inventor
Henry Wehrhahn
By his Attorney J. W. Harden

I must give special thanks to Mr. Bob Malcolm and Mr. Tom Phelps who have been of immense help in the preparation of this book. Colleen Borrie kindly took on the task of copyediting and made many improvements to the text. I also wish to thank Mr. Owen Aiken, Sahil Bagga, André Grahl, Mr Laurence Cooper, Jillian Hayward, Marisha Karwa, Mr Dave Marden, Eleanor McDonald, Marianne Plasmans-Damen, and Dr. David Selner, and Mr Rowan Taylor. I am particularly grateful to Anne Schneeberger for designing the book. Her skills and patience were very much appreciated.

A preliminary article in the *New Zealand Memories* magazine about milk cans (with an invitation to send me information) prompted a 'flood' of letters over many months. I am very grateful to those people who kindly took the trouble to write to me. Other articles such as those in the Australian Magazine *'Antique Collecting for Pleasure and Profit'* and the Mumbai based Newspaper *'Daily News & Analysis'* prompted similar responses.

The research for this book has raised more questions than answers. I don't have all the answers. Indeed throughout this book there are questions and uncertainties. I encourage readers to contact me should they have new information but also particularly if they are able to correct anything that I have written.

I have made every reasonable effort to contact the copyright holders of the images. I apologize if there are any omissions and would be pleased to insert the appropriate acknowledgments in any subsequent editions.

This book is in two parts plus appendices. Part one is a brief account of the history of milk cans, their shape and design, their role in society and how the design has been an inspiration to artists and designers. Part two is a compendium of milk can images.

Volumes are expressed in Imperial Units (not USA) and weights in pounds (lbs.) Metric equivalents are provided. Conversion factors are in the appendices.

◀ *Soldering the lower band on an English milk churn (Circa 1922, England). Photograph courtesy of Bob Malcolm*

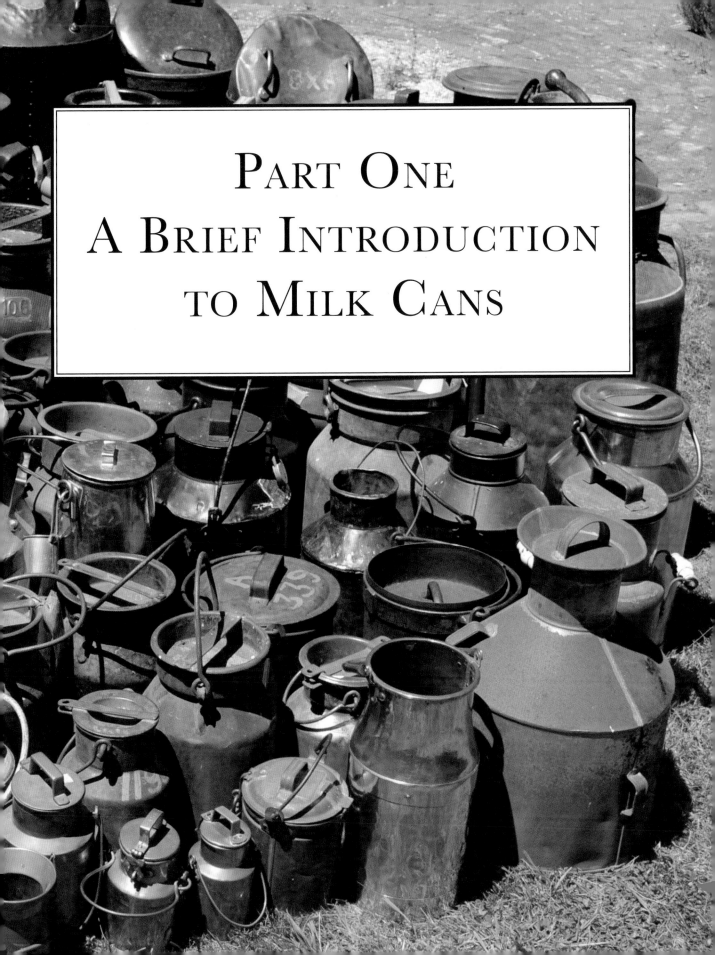

PART ONE
A BRIEF INTRODUCTION
TO MILK CANS

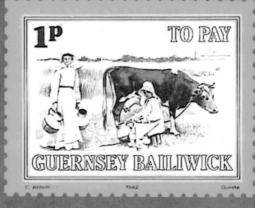

▲ *Milk cans and a milk pail celebrated on postage stamps.*

HISTORY AND DESIGN

The term 'milk can' is of course found in many languages. For example: bidon de lait (French), melkbus or melk kan (Dutch), una lata de leche or una lechera (Spanish), milchkanne (German), una latta di latte or bidones da latte (Italian), maelk kan (Danish), leite pode (Portugese), moloko mozhet (Russian), and gall llaeth (Welsh).

In English, familiar terms include milk can, milk churn, cream can, milk pail and dairy can. The difference between a 'milk can' and a 'cream can' appears not to be well defined. Some retired farmers have said to me that 'small cans' were for cream and 'large cans 'straight sided cans' were used for taking milk to the local cheese factory. These were later returned to the farm containing whey for the pigs. Apparently 'tapered cans' were used to send cream to the butter factory.

For the purpose of this book I use the term 'milk can'. I define 'milk can' as a container (usually with a lid) commonly made of metal and used for carrying or transporting milk or cream (from cows, buffaloes and other domestic animals). This includes small hand-held containers (up to about two pints) once commonly used by members of the household. It does not include milk jugs or milk bottles.

Household containers for holding milk or cream have included milk bottles (glass, cardboard and plastic), milk jugs, and milk vases. Other terms include 'milk pots', and 'creamers'. Names for early containers for transporting milk or cream and later used in the farm dairy included 'milk pitchers', 'milk buckets' and 'milk pails.

What did the earliest containers for milk look like? More than 6,000 years ago someone sculptured a frieze. Thomas Ross Pirtle (1870-1938), in his general outline of dairying (when referring to one of the oldest buildings excavated near Babylon by the British Museum and the Museum of Philadelphia, U.S.A) made the following observation:

"The most interesting, a panel four feet long, has on one side a milking scene, cows and their calves and men milking the cows into tall jars".

In a footnote, Pirtle noted that the 'jars' were similar in shape to those in England now called 'churns' used to hold milk brought from the farms.

European farmers may also have begun dairying activities as long as 6,000 years. This has been concluded from the analysis of degraded fats on fragments of pottery dating back to Neolithic Britain.

In southern England, archaeologists at Stonehenge (which dates back to 3,200 B.C.) have uncovered fragments of pots which once stored meat and dairy products.

An extraordinary exhibit in the Brooklyn Museum (U.S.A.) is an Egyptian milk vase dating from circa 1500-1400 B.C. Made of clay and measuring just under 14 inches tall and 3 ¾ inches wide, this vessel is in the shape of a women's head, arms and breasts. Unusual in shape, this may have been used for breast milk from a woman who had given birth to a male child.

Metal milk cans have been made in many parts of the world for at least one thousand years. For example, on the Island of Guernsey (one of the Channel Islands off the coast of France), the traditional round copper milk can has been made for over 1,000 years. Originally made of tin-plated steel, the shape provides strength and there is less slopping of the milk. There is little documentation about how they were originally made because most details were passed from master to apprentice. They were originally hammered out in the open using a tree stump in the same way that armour was made. They were still in use in the first half of the 20th century. Locally called milk jugs, effective sizes ranged from a half pint up to a gallon. Some cans were made up to five gallons. The standard Guernsey measure was a 'pot' and held about four pints.

Another very old design is the brass (pital) milk pots used in Rajasthan, India. The practice of women carrying the pots on their heads goes back centuries and is still practiced today. These brass pots are still made today but many families have handed down these pots from generation to generation.

Informative milk can images can be found amongst paintings by artists such as Jan Steen (1625-1679) and Martin Drolling (1752-1817). A Lovely painting by James Ward shows a man riding a donkey with a reasonably large metal can (approximately six gallons) on the side of the animal. This image is included by G.E. Fussell in his book *The English Dairy Farmer* and describes the image as *'Modern Milk Transport in 1800'*.

One name in particular stands out in connection with the sale of dairy utensils and that was Mr. George Barham (1836-1913). In London he established the Dairy Supply Company. He was concerned about adulterated milk and the way it was transported and subsequently developed the modern milk churn and also methods for cooling the milk. Furthermore he was instrumental in introducing modern dairy practices to India.

Think milk cans and think India. There is probably no other country that has such a long history of making and using milk cans. Indeed, when researching for this book, India cropped up again and again. This is not surprising because in India milk is not just a commodity. Milk has a special significance dates back to Hindu mythology. India is now the world's largest producer of milk. On the 26th of November, India celebrates the birthday of the legendary Dr. Verghese Kurien as National Milk Day.

A 'typical' metal milk can and specialist cans from the early twentieth century

In countries such as the U.S.A., Britain, Australia, and New Zealand, a 'typical' example of a milk cans from the 1940s would have been between six and ten gallons made from galvanised (tinned) steel. They had straight sides, slightly narrow necks and a tight-fitting lids or covers which were made specifically for each can. Early cans were riveted while the later steel cans were seamless.

There have been many different designs for milk can lids. For example in 1921 *Grayson's Dairy Utensils* catalogue offered three kinds; (the 'hygienic No. 1' dust and rain-proof cover', the 'hygienic No. 2' dust and rain-proof cover', and the 'Plain or London' cover.)

In the 1930's some were designed with a rounded (mushroom top) so as not to catch water in the lid. Some lids were made to fit over the base of the can while other lids fitted neatly into the body of the can. In some instances there were two lids, one of which would sink down in the liquid to prevent the liquid from being agitated. Such lids were not easy to remove because of the suction. Some patents have been issued for improvements to the shape of milk can lids.

Not all cans were fitted with lids. Early nineteenth century and late eighteenth century paintings show brass dairy cans that could not possibly have been fitted with lids because of the 'flared' shape of the can's neck.

The handles usually projected from the can, presumably to make them easy to grip. There have been many different designs for the handles, some of which were designed (and patented) to cause the least damage when the cans collided with one another. For example, the 1921 *Dairy Utensils Catalogue* from T. Grayson offered three designs (The 'Everest' soldered on to the body of the can, 'drop' or 'fall down' handles, and the 'ordinary or 'upright' handle). The can's top and was strengthened with a steel band. There were provisions for locking the lid to the can with a padlock. Locked small cans presumably helped to prevent the theft of milk. Locked delivery cans with a bottom tap helped to mitigate dishonesty of watering down the contents.

The painted numbers (supply number) and letters were the same on the lid and the can. There was a brass lozenge (badge) with the name of the dairy farm and the name of the dairy factory. Not many examples exist today but a few survive complete with brass lozenges.

Several designs included a tap for draining milk from the can. A less common feature was a spout for pouring milk.

Specialist cans include those that were made or modified to be cream gravity separator cans. Sometimes called 'deep setting cans' these were usually tall and slim with a 'window' on the side to measure the cream. Some had a centre column for cold water to cool the milk. Another group are 'milker' cans or 'surge milkers'. The surge bucket milker was invented in 1922 by Herbert McCormack. He was awarded at least 50 U.S.A. patents. This bucket or 'can' hung under the cow suspended by a steel spring attached to a leather strap over the cow's back. Hugely successful, the surge bucket milker exceeded all expectations History of the Surge Bucket Milker 1922-1999. http://www.surgemilker.com/history.html accessed March 2017.

Perhaps the most unusual specialist can was the pneumatic can used to ensure that milk was not contaminated. Compressed air is pumped into the can until the lid was locked. On opening a valve, the milk is forced out.

Manufacture of steel dairy cans

There appear to be very few records from the late 19th Century and early 20th Century about the manufacture of milk cans. Photographs of cans being made are very scarce. Initially milk cans were made by local tinsmiths and general metal workers. In 1883, a London tinsmith by the name of Mr. Higginbotham took Mr. Harry Hale on as an apprentice tinsmith. An interview in 1930 with Mr. Hale revealed much about the arduous hours. "In my early days we worked from 8:00 a.m. to 8:00 p.m. The work included making utensils all by hand ranging from a tiny two pence cream can to the 17 gallon churns". He explained that there was a class distinction in Victorian times amongst tinsmiths, with the churn makers considering themselves the 'aristocrats' of the trade. They supported their title by wearing top hats, smoked clay pipes and refused to associate with those who were merely makers of small cans.

The manufacture of milk cans for some businesses was just one small part of many other activities. For example, in 1905, a Mr. George Dyer & Co. advertised his business (certified by London City & Guilds Science and Art Department) as being "Sanitary Plumbers, Gasfitters, Sheet and Metal workers – with estimates given for tanks, milk cans and dairy utensils as a speciality".

Most unusual was the supply of milk can kit-sets! The Buhl Stamping Co. In the USA offered the five components of a milk can that could be assembled in four operations. According to the instructions, "a boy can make up this can."

Some milk cans were modified cans such as 'billycans'. Billycans are not only associated with Australia but also the U.K. and Ireland. In Canada the term is a billy pot. It is highly unlikely that 'homemade' cans would have been subject to any design standards (with the risk of lead poisoning (if too much solder was used) whereas the cans made in factories would have been, and still are, made to specified standards milk can standards. For example, in the 1930s *The International Dairy Congress* set up a committee to engage in standardizing milk bottles and milk cans. A few years later, the same Congress addressed the question of standardizing the alloy cans that were slowly replacing galvanized cans.

The problems arising from non-standardised cans was very well argued in Australia in 1944. Newspapers reported that "complaints had been received by The Standards Association about faulty tinning, lack of uniformity in design, unsatisfactory design to withstand rough handling, lack of interchangeability of lids, ill-fitting lids, top rim and handles badly fitted to the body of the can, and general mechanical faults".

One illustrated account of the manufacture of welded milk cans appeared in a 1953 issue of the journal *New Zealand Engineering*. Written by a former employee (S.F. Crewther) of a milk can manufacturer (Hardleys of Auckland) the article included the following: "Originally cans were made from tinned steel sheet with riveted and soldered seams. Being hand-made, great difficulty was experienced in maintaining a standard size to allow lids to be interchangeable. Then came the gas-welded can, which was hand-hammered, and an improvement on the old methods. High grade 18 gauge mild steel is used. After first being cut to size, the sheet is rolled to a cylindrical shape, and the longitudinal seam spot-welded. The seam is then passed through the seam welder. Next, the cylinder has the bottom spot and seam welded. It is then slipped over a cylindrical chuck of a big lathe and pressure is applied to a free running roller. This smooths out the welded seams and 'rounds up' the can. The can is then mounted in a spinning lathe reducing the can neck from approximately 14 inches to ten inches diameter. The can is then ready for the tinning shop. Lids, which have been stamped out in a press and then tinned, are fitted." Of all the stages in the manufacture of the cans, it was widely thought that the tinning of the cans was the most important process.

Dairies

Factories that made milk products such as condensed milk or chocolate often had their own 'branded' dairy cans. Cadbury milk cans and Carnation milk cans are just two examples from Britain and the USA respectively. Also in the U.S.A. the Hershey Chocolate Company used a fairly standard dairy can.

Dairy companies and dairy supply companies were the main manufactures of milk cans. However, the term 'dairy' has several meanings. It has been used to refer to the 'farm dairy' where a few cows were milked and a separator was used to take off the cream. It was not uncommon for a dairy factory or creamery (that processed the milk brought from the farms) to be called a 'dairy. In some countries the corner grocery shop was called 'the dairy'.

In the U.K. the origin of many dairy companies and dairy shops was the cow keeper. For example in 1819 a cow keeper by the name of William Porter started a business in Middlesex which was later to become Job's Dairy. A cow keeper is defined as "someone who kept one or more cows (a common source of livelihood) when a cow was kept in the backyard of a house, providing milk which was sold at the front door or window, forerunner of the local dairy". http://www.worldthroughthelens.com/family-history/old-occupations.php (October 2016). An 1825 painting by George Scharf shows an example of a house where cows were milked on the premises and the milk sold.

Some dairy shops have become an international sensation. In 1879, Paul Gustav Leander Pfund went to Dresden to establish a dairy to meet the increasing demand for fully hygienic milk. His shop was established in 1880 and is extensively decorated with beautifully hand painted tiles. It is not surprising that Pfund's dairy is registered in the Guinness Book of Records as the most 'beautiful dairy shop in the world!' That the City of Dresden claimed to have one of the largest and best milk distributing establishments in Germany was reported in 1909 at the 35th Annual Meeting of the Illinois State Dairymen's Association.

In the 1860s, many Welsh owned dairies were established along the roads leading to Paddington Railway Station. This was a result of a combination of new railways and hard times for Welsh farmers. The Tower Bridge Dairy owned by D. Davies & Son (dairy farmers) was just one example.

In 1864, Mr. George Barham founded the Express Country Milk Supply Co. This was at a time when milk was beginning to be brought from the country to the London by rail. He is also credited with inventing the railway milk churn based on the conical design of the wooden butter churn. He launched the Dairy Supply Company, and the exquisite building (built in 1888) still stands in Coptic Street London. High on one wall is the red-brick relief of a beribboned milk churn. The building is now occupied by PizzaExpress. Anyone remotely interested in the history and design of dairy cans would surely wish to spend time at what was once the major centre for dairy supplies. In the late nineteenth century they published many trade catalogues under the titles of 'Dairy Machinery and Appliances' and 'Dairy Utensils'.

Included in some catalogues were dairy related utensils such as glass tumblers and china drinking horns. Ornaments, bowls, flower pots and tiles were also advertised.

By 1880 there were 14 dairy companies in London (Whetham, 1964) and much variation in the nature of their business. For example, by this time George Barham had set up The Dairy Supply Company. The Amalgamated Dairies was describing itself as a wholesaler. The Aylesbury Dairy Company had shops in Bayswater supplied from its Horsham dairy and from cowstalls in Portobello Road. Meanwhile, Tunks and Tisdall kept their old fashioned partnership and the old fashioned title of 'cow keepers' for their Holland Park Dairy.

Other dairy company suppliers from around the world include the Oneonta Dairy Company (ODC) and The Buhl Stamping Co., both in the USA. In Australia, F. Malleys & Sons Ltd. was established in 1884 and they made the well-known 'Sunrise' milk cans. In New Zealand, a Mr. Alex Harvey (tinsmith) arrived in Auckland in 1886 and established Alex Harvey & Sons Ltd. They were the main manufacturer of milk cans in New Zealand. The Company became well known not only for their 'R.V.' and 'Ideal' seamless milk cans but also for their colour printing on tin.

Materials

For centuries, milk containers have been made from clay and also from animal skins (e.g. the qirbah or milk/water bag used in many countries such as Asia, Arabia and Oman). In Bhutan they were made from bamboo. In Europe, early milk containers were made of wood, later to be replaced by ceramic containers and metal containers.

In the late nineteenth century and early twentieth century ceramic 'counter' pans that held milk were either for sale in a general store or were used in the home dairies of aristocratic households. Among the most celebrated makers was W.T. Copeland & Sons in Staffordshire, England. One of their catalogues includes hand-held milk cans with can handles, milk pans, and counter pans made from both china and tin. An example of a Circa 1910 counter pan (by Malings, a very successful pottery in Newcastle) was shown on the BBC Antiques Roadshow (Hartland Abby 1, on January 1, 2012). That is probably the only dairy 'can' ever seen on the BBC Antiques Roadshow.

Brass (tinned on the inside) has been a very popular metal for making dairy cans. Some examples have survived hundreds of years of use. Copper cans were made primarily for their anti-microbial properties and started to appear from about the 1920s when scientists were beginning to become aware of these properties in copper. Victorian milk cans were rarely made of copper although some had copper plate on the outside.

Most milk cans were made of tinned or galvanized iron or steel. In 1880, an advertisement in the London Daily News reported "The most important Invention of the Year connected with dairying is the application of Bessemer Steel to the manufacture of dairy utensils and may be seen at the Dairy Supply Company". The Bessemer process was the first inexpensive industrial process for the mass-production of steel.

Later, there were stainless steel and aluminium cans. Despite the reference to 'can' (a metal vessel) other materials included glass (with a protective outer layer) and various forms of plastic were used.

Modern plastic milk cans are widely made in India and are now available in many countries including the U.S.A. and the U.K. The following is a personal communication from a senior journalist in India; "I've been in India since the Magadh Empire; milk cans have been made from bronze, copper, brass, stainless steel, aluminium and now plastic – in the most god-awful fluorescent colours!"

Volume and shape

In mid-19th century London, there was a unit of volume known as the 'barn gallon' (equal to 17 pints). Eight barn gallons (of 17 imperial pints each) or 17 gallons was, for a while, the standard unit for iron railway milk churns. Whetham (1964) wrote that this unit seems to have been derived from the old custom of the seller adding one gill (1/4 pint) for each imperial gallon, to allow for spillage and wastage. The volumes of these hand-made iron churns was not stamped on the churns and they did not stand up to rough handling, they were liable to leak and became rusty.

The amount of milk in each churn could vary from day to day because of the dents they received on the journey. The deficiencies in volume of the churns, nominally holding 17 gallons, was as much as three pints. It was also reported that the condition of fresh milk was expansive and took an hour or two to settle down. This also made a difference to the quantity of the milk.

A report in *The Cowkeeper and Dairyman's Journal* of 1888 noted that farmers in Buckinghamshire (England) were having discussions about the verdant question of gauges for churns and wished to have an exact imperial measure. That discussion seemed to last for several years because in England it was reported in 1906 that some farmers were still using milk churns that held eight barn gallons.

By 1880, the London Dairy Supply Company was offering a 17 gallon milk churn from double-tinned steel plate, with a lid designed to keep out dust ad rain, as a cheaper and more durable product. At that time the Dairy Supply Company also advertised many sizes of the different types of milk cans. For small cans the common unit of volume was a quart. Hand cans (they were clipped to the side of a hand-cart) ranged in volume from 6 quarts (1.5 gallons) to as small as ½ gill (1/8th pint). In 1909, this small volume of milk (or cream) was noted in America in a report to the Illinois State Dairymen's Association at their 35th Annual Meeting. The report read "these tin pails are delivered to the customer in the same way that we sell milk bottles. Some of the pails hold only an ounce. They represent the smallest quantity of a dairy product that I have ever seen."

'Bottles' (cans for conveying milk or cream by road or rail) ranged in volume from one quart to 30 quarts (7.5 gallons). Hand-held Kettles (small hand cans that were clipped to kettles) ranged in size from six quarts to 14 quarts. The larger examples had internal rims to prevent spillage in the carts. Carriers' pails ranged in volume for 12 quarts to 20 quarts. Retail delivery churns ranged in volume from 40 quarts (ten gallons) to 62 quarts (15.5 gallons). The railway milk churns (cans) ranged in volume from 34 quarts - or four Barn gallons - to 68 quarts or eight Barn gallons (17 gallons). In 1900, the 17 gallon (conical) railway milk churn was the most common size.

The diversity of sizes and shapes offered by the London Dairy Supply Co. was particularly impressive. Presumably each type of can had a specific use. Not all milk cans were used by milkmen on carts. Hotels, railways, etc., must have had their own 'on site' cans so perhaps there were different designs adapted for that purpose

Equally diverse in design were the 20 or so different cans made by the Buhl Stamping Co. (Detroit, Chicago). The names of the different designs included 'Philadelphia'. 'Baltimore', 'city delivery', 'Sunlight', 'Sunset', 'Eastern', 'Jersey', 'Chicago' and 'Western'.

Delivery tanks much larger than 17 gallons were used in other countries. For example, a milk tank on a two-wheeled cart was used in Holland and would have held at least 20 gallons. In Italy, tanks holding about 150 gallons were transported on horse-drawn carts for milk delivery to local shops. The milk was decanted into buckets.

Ornamental show churns for display in shop windows (advertising fresh milk) ranged in height from 12 inches to 21 inches. The smaller versions advertised milk for children or for invalids. Show cans were also available from ½ pint to three quarts.

The ten gallon milk cans and five gallon milk cans, familiar to older generations in Britain, were introduced in the 1930's and used until the 1970's. Household dairy cans were typically much smaller and held no more than a few pints.

Shapes of milk cans vary around the world. That fact was noted in 1909 in a report to the *Illinois State Dairymen's Association* that read "There is not much difference in the shape of our cans … but going from one country to another the size and shape of milk cans is striking. Brass cans are common in Holland. In England they are called 'churns'. In Switzerland milk cans are made in the shape of a knapsack. A person interested in making collections could easily find enjoyment in getting together the many different types of milk cans that are used in different countries".

An 1862 painting by the French artist Jean-Francois Millet shows a woman pouring water into a spherically shaped dairy can. Indeed, the spherical shape has long proved to be popular in countries as far apart as India and the Island of Guernsey.

The shape of milk cans up to ten gallons was typically straight sides with conical shoulders and a short straight neck. Greater than ten gallons, the shape was typically conical because that provided greater stability.

Amongst the collections at The National Museum of American History there are some very simple shaped tinned steel milk cans. From the 1875-1900 period, they vary in size from two pints to three U.S. gallons. Most are made from five pieces of metal, all joined by soldered folded seams. The handles are made of straps of metal with wire reinforcement rolled under the edges. The cans have straight sides, a conical shoulder and a straight neck.

The same simple shape for a tin milk can also appears to have been used in Wales, U.K. Two examples (two imperial pints and 12 imperial pints) look very similar to the examples in The National Museum of American History. A clue as to their Welsh connection comes in the form of a small (4 inches, 10.2 cm. tall) Goss Ware milk can ornament of the same shape. The base mark reads 'model of a 'Welsh Jack'. Were these simple tinned milk cans in Wales called 'Welsh Jacks?' To make matters even more mysterious, in a 1977 article in the magazine *Antiques & Art*, the author mentions "the St. David's Can" and goes on to say "the more rarely seen, St. David's can was the favourite utensil of the Welsh dairies (Roberts, 1977, Bygones from the Dairy, *Antiques & Art*, 1977). No further information can be found.

Another shape is the 'milk pitcher' or 'water pitcher'. This was used in many locations such as Persia (for collecting goat's milk) and also in France. Perhaps the most unusual shape was the square milk can (there were also square milk bottles) which were extensively used in a few countries such as France, England and Argentina. A 1944 article in *Popular Mechanics* reported that "square milk bottles developed by the Owen-Illinois Glass Co., save 20-50 percent in storage space".

PROMOTING AND ADVERTISING MILK CANS

In the early 1900s, hardware merchants such as The Charles Williams Stores (New York), Hibbard, Spencer, Nartlett & Co. (Chicago), the Shapleigh Hardware Company (St.Louis), and Wood, Alexander & James, Ltd. (Canada) advertised dairy supplies in their respective trade catalogues.

Advertisements from early twentieth century periodicals tell us more about the diversity in shapes. The language used to promote the qualities of the cans is typical of the marketing of the day. This for example from the Charles Williams Stores 1913 Catalogue: " The highest grade steel plate is used; rivet holes are punched and then tinned and re-tinned, leaving no parts to rust and making the most perfect can it is possible to produce. Different manufacturers have different names for the same style of can. We believe our customers will have no difficulty in identifying our cans with the style of can which they prefer".

Catalogues from around 1900 produced by the Dairy Supply Company in London are possibly the most informative sources about dairy utensils, machinery and appliances.

In Britain, department stores such as the Army and Navy store included advertisements for dairy utensils in their catalogues from around 1907 onwards. Interestingly they use the term 'cream bottles' when referring to tinned steel containers ranging from one to three pints.

Some of the most interesting examples of dairy can and dairy utensils ephemera are the illustrated catalogues produced by can manufacturers and dairy companies alike. In New Zealand, dairy can catalogues from Alex Harvey & Sons Ltd. were regarded as outstanding examples of graphic design.

In the USA, The Buhl Stamping Co. (Detroit, Chicago) produced a variety of ephemera including a little booklet apply called *A Study in Milk Cans*'. Published in 1898, this booklet contained illustrations of many different types of milk cans and advice to enable salesmen to sell the best milk cans. Included in a list of ten selling suggestions there was the following: "Make any tests you please at our expense. Drop a Buhl Can on its head down an elevator shaft and show your customer that it will not crack or leak. Batter one against a common can and note the result, or scrape the tin off with a knife and see the thickness of the coating. Note the smooth soldering, within and without, of all Buhl made-up Cans".

In addition to dairy cans and utensils being widely advertised in trade catalogues, some milk cans were specifically designed to advertise the sale of milk. Some very fine decorative ceramic examples (show cans) were made to stand in dairy shop windows.

Promotional materials issued by some dairies and dairy associations included match holders and sets of cards. For example, French's Dairy in Rugby Street, London (the oldest dairy in London) gave away nickel plated brass vesta cases (match cases). In New Zealand, the South Island Dairy Association also issued complimentary metal matchboxes. As recently as 1965, Clover Dairies Ltd., produced a series of 25 cards on 'The Story of Milk' which show milk cans being used, transported and washed.

PATENTS FOR MILK CANS AND A REGISTERED DESIGN

Many patents have been taken out for improvements in milk cans and dairy can accessories. For example, 543 patents were issued in the USA between 1859 and 1919, most of which were from US citizens. One particularly interesting example from 1910 is a patent for a glass-lined milk can. There is provision for the lining to be "readily and quickly replaced".

Perhaps the most novel patent was for a milk can designed to collect the milk directly from the cow. The can was placed on its side and the milk was directed from the cow into the can. Measuring the volume of milk was simplified by attaching a meter that recorded the volume or attaching an external graduated tube. Some patents addressed the problem of keeping the contents cool so those were issued for insulating the cans by insulation jackets and applying ice in or around the cans. Another popular idea was to stop the milk moving in the can and so prevent agitation of the contents. This could be achieved by increasing the pressure in the can by lowering an inner lid into the can. Conversely, some patents were for methods ways of ventilating the contents. Preventing the adulteration of the contents also occupied the minds of most inventors. Suitable devices range from complex locks and keys built into the lid to lockable boxes (safes) rather like letter boxes. The design of the lids (including closing mechanisms) and handles elicited some patents; with one lid design including a tag holder or identification number.

There were patents for removable handles and for a handle that made less noise when it was dropped against the can. In July 1910 the question was debated in a Paris court whether morning rattling of milk cans was a disturbance of the peace or a necessary sound! The court concluded that the dairyman must move his milk cans without creating a nuisance.

Pouring mechanisms prompted many patents as did integral agitators for mixing the contents prior to pouring. Related patents were for cleaning the cans and removing the dents.

Not surprisingly there were many patented transportation devices for cans, for loading cans on to vehicles and also for securing the cans on vehicles.

Finally, while patents were issued for milk cans, there was at least one registered design for a milk can ornaments. Boulogne-sur-mer (France) is famous for its many forms of cheeses (fromages). This is the lovely Goss Crested China Boulogne dairy can. The design was registered in London in 1909.

 # ACCESSORIES

One simple accessory was the funnel. Illustrations in some old dairy handbooks show that funnels (in the shape of an upturned bottomless dairy can) were used when pouring milk from bucket to can.

Keeping milk cool was of prime importance. One basic method was to stand full milk cans in water. By 1870, Lawrence's patent capillary milk-cooler became widely adopted (Whetham, 1964). This consisted of a zigzag of metal tubes through which water circulated and over which milk was poured. The patent was awarded five medals between 1872 and 1874.

Later, watertight cylinders (filled with crushed ice and screwed into the can's shoulder) were employed. Similar to this method was the milk can water cooler (including the Ashland Kuhler milk can cooler). This was immersed in the can. Water flowed through stainless steel tubing to cool the milk. Also similar was the 'temperature can' used for cooling or warming cream to the 'proper' temperature for churning. The Dairy Supply Company of London sold two sizes, one for medium cans and one the other larger cans.

In the 1950s, 'Prestcold' advertised 'churn immersion milk coolers' which consisted of a chest cooler with a manual hoist attached for moving cans in and out of the coolers. A simpler arrangement was to use a cooling unit with doors opening at floor level

Insulation jackets for milk cans were not unusual but few examples survive. The most beautiful examples were made of wood while other examples such as those made by The Dairy Supply Co., London were simple insulated canvas jackets.

Other insulation methods included milk cans that rested in water troughs and also the age-old use of mud pots (porous earthenware pots with a container for the milk).

Common accessories were milk scales to check a cow's production, dairy thermometers, milk samplers, skimmers (fleeters) for separating the cream, and dippers (milk measures) for ladling the milk into smaller containers. One unusual milk device was a 'bottle filling' measure with a funnel spout. These were made by R. & A. Lister and Co., England.

There were also syles (dairy strainers or soiling dishes). These were wooden or ceramic bowls with the base cut out; when in use the base was covered with a linen mesh that filtered the milk to remove grit, cow hairs and bovine dandruff.

Other accessories included lead seals and pincers, taps for some milk cans, measuring sticks, ice chambers, plungers or stirring rods, wooden or leather mallets to remove or replace lids, milking stools, strainers for use when pouring milk from bucket to can, and cream separating pans used prior to skimming off the cream. Milk boxes could also be included. These were insulated tin boxes that stood in the porch of a house or on the veranda for temporary storage of milk and dairy deliveries.

PROCESSING AND MAINTENANCE

The very early local dairy factories (creameries) used hoists of various kinds to lift the cans from the carts for weighing. Specially made iron grappling hooks were employed to lift the cans. Later, when milk lorries were used, the cans were wheeled off the lorry decks on to a loading bay. Cans were unloaded in order of collection on to the steel-lined stages, some of which had a ridge running along them for easy movement of the cans. Once inside the cool interior of the factories, there would be an incessant clanking of metal cans. Lids were removed, scraped and put on a conveyor in the same order as the cans were tipped. Can contents were graded, weighed and poured into a vat. The tare weight of the can (inscribed on the brass plate on its side) was deducted from the total weight. The empty cans would then move along a conveyor through a washer. Later the same cans would be returned back to the farm.

The following useful description about the reception of milk cans is from E.L. Crossley's 1959 book *The United Kingdom Dairy Industry:*

"After unloading the cans on to the reception dock, all milk is examined and sampled at regular periods. The cans are then conveyed to a weighing machine, where the milk is tipped and the quantity recorded. Shortage of labour and the need to increase the speed and reduce the physical effort of handling increasing quantities of milk has led to extensive mechanization. Usually the cans are taken by a power-driven rising conveyor from the edge of the dock to a convenient height for tipping and loading the empty cans into a can washer. At the beginning they pass through a lid-loosening device. The empty cans are passed over a stainless-steel draining rack to the can-washing machine. At small dairies, the can washer may be of the rotary type. At larger dairies, straight-through tunnel-type washers are employed. The cans and lids are passed automatically into the machine and discharged at the opposite end, inversion of the washed can and replacement of the lid is performed mechanically".

At a time when the typical dairy cans of the 1940s were the main containers for transporting milk and cream, there was a need to re-tin and repair the cans. The British Ministry of Agriculture made an appeal to the milk industry to take special care of milk churns in order to save steel. They appealed to all users of churns to see that re-tinning and repairs such as new bottoms, handles, etc., were carried out as soon as necessary so that the purchase of new churns could be kept to a minimum.

This work was sometimes undertaken by sheet-metal workshops or engineering shops. As the cows were dried off and the dairy season ended, dairy cans would arrive in the yards of the sheet-metal workshops. They would be stacked 6 or 7 cans high across the yard. Prior to re-tinning, the top and bottom hoops were removed, then to remove any dents, the body of the can was put through a whaling machine. This machine was similar to that used by panel beaters to reshape mudguards and panels. The cans would then be re-tinned and the hoops replaced and soldered on. The bottom hoops were often very worn and therefore had to be replaced more often.

THE FARM DAIRY AND SOCIAL ASPECTS

Before the collection of milk cans from the farm gate became the usual practice, some farmers would take the cans direct to the dairy factories. A retired 98 year old dairy farmer (Owen) wrote "After the milk factory workers had winched the can out of your cart so that it swung clear, they would then swing it across to the cheese vat. The can had some lugs located below the can's halfway point so that there was more weight in the upper part of the can. The milk would shoot out of the can into the vat. Then you would take the empty cans back, fill them up with whey (water extracted from the cheese) and feed this to your pigs back on the farm".

"We used to wash the milk cans with hot water and caustic soda. We boiled up a copper, especially to wash the cans out."

In the really early days they used to have skimming pans where they put the fresh milk so that the cream would settle at the top. They were like a huge ladle full of little holes so that thin cream and milk would run through. The thick cream was used to make butter".

A typical 6 gallon milk can when full would have weighed about 62 lbs (28 kgs). A full ten gallon can weighed about 103 lbs (47 kgs). There would have been required considerable strength and skills to handle cans larger than ten gallons and to reel them across the ground or floor. One correspondent noted that the 20 gallon cans were a 'b…..' to move!

Rolling (reeling) a full milk can was one of many aspects of farmcraft mentioned and illustrated in the 1942 *A Book of FarmCraft* by Michael Greenhill and Evelyn Dunbar. Seemingly a basic task, their book was written during World War two when farming relied more and more on the work of novices – people who were doing farm-work for the first time in their lives.

The full can would be taken from the dairy shed to the farm gate collection point by various means. Some farms had a small trolley (platform on wheels) which ran along metal rails. Gravity helped move the trolley to the gate and then someone had to push the trolley back to the milking shed.

Other simple solutions on the farm included a simple metal home-made wheelbarrow or hand cart, or a horse drawn sledge or tractor drawn cart.

At the farm gate there was a milk can stand (loading dock). Very few survive today but dairy can stands at farm gates were once (like milestones) common landscape features along many country roads. They were designed so that the cans could easily be reeled off the stand on to a cart or lorry (dairy can collections often resulted in strained muscles and even hernias). These stands were built from wood, bricks or stone and some had roofs. Most accommodated between four and six milk cans. A few were built like a small school theatre stage. Ingenious designs included those made of a cart wheel on its side so that a can could be easily rotated. Some surviving milk stands now receive only mail deliveries.

Historical societies such as the Llanteg History Society in Wales have recorded the location and condition of many of the surviving milk can stands. The artist William Tillyer was so taken by milk can stands that he prepared a collection of photographs *(The Furnished Landscape (milk stands); photographed in the North York Moors National Park)*. He wrote; "One reason for making these photographs was that I found people seemed to be unaware of the beauty and significance of these structures in the landscape. After all they were humdrum make do affairs, their function was paramount and masked their beauty. They were treated beyond consideration. Expectation before their physical reality where presence is put into a passive mode while expectation and function takes precedence. Like the Skellig Rocks, signal rather than light form and space are paramount. Psychology and seeing become as close as Jekyll and Hyde. They are inseparable."

When placed on the stand of the loading dock, lids were left slightly open to allow air to circulate and stop the cream from going sour. However there was a risk. During periods of darkness, rats were known to sample the contents by dipping then licking their tails. From time to time birds could find their way into the cans and sometimes drown. It was common practice for the milk trucks to check the cans for birds and any debris.

The journey from the farms to the local factory or creamery was sometimes referred to as the 'billy can run'. At the dairy factories there were specially designed hand barrows or trolleys and also conveyor belts for the cans.

The number of cans used by each farm depended on the size of the dairy herd (sometimes only 3-5 cows) and the frequency of collection. It was not uncommon practice for farms to have two complete sets of milk cans. One set would be filled and sent to the dairy factory and returned the next day while the other set had been filled and was ready for collection. Whatever the number, it was a very special occasion for farming families when the first, brand-new dairy can was delivered to the farm. A few photographs survive showing proud families with their new dairy can. Such occasions were obviously thought to be worth recording, as were children playing with dairy cans.

In Canada, the trucks were driven by 'milk haulers'. The book by K. Jane Watt (Milk Stories) published in 2000, includes first-hand accounts of the challenges and rewards of 'milk hauling' in British Columbia. Collections and deliveries were made every day including Christmas day. One milk hauler recalled that the milk truck dictated the lives of a lot of farmers in that everything revolved around what time the milk track arrived. Furthermore, the milk haulers got to know every family as the children grew up.

The cans were not only used for transporting cream or milk. Some cans were used to send milk to the local cheese factory and were returned full of whey for the farm pigs. Other cans were used to send cream to the butter factory. After cleaning at the factory, the cans would be returned to the farm with a ticket inside on which was recorded the condition and amount of cream that had been received. There might also have been a pound or so of butter enclosed, as ordered by the farm. The lorry drivers and dairy cans served as a means of communication between the farm and the local dairy factory and village shops. Doctor's prescriptions were also collected and delivered by the drivers. Occasionally messages were scratched on to the inside of can lids so that information could be communicated to other farmers. Smuggling illicit whisky bottles in cans was occasionally reported.

A news report from Australia in 1953 is headed 'Sending Milk Can Mail'. The article describes "the milk can as an important part of communication in the dairy industry" and is accompanied by a photograph of two women putting official notes into cans to be returned to farmers.

In the U.K. by the 1950s, collection of milk cans had to cater for an extremely large number of farms. The following is an extract from E.L. Crossley's book *The United Kingdom Dairy Industry:* "The bulk of the milk supply is collected in cans of 10 gallon (45.4 l) capacity, and much attention has been devoted to standardization of both vehicles and cans; improved loading resulting from this has also played an important part in reducing transport costs. Collection vehicles are designed specifically for milk transport, of suitable dimensions to carry a definite number of standard cans, which are designed to give the maximum loading on the deck. A British Standard specification for milk cans has greatly eased the problems of transport and handling of cans. This standard design, the subject of much study by engineers and dairymen, is a vertical –sided type with a conical shoulder. Apart from good standards of construction, it incorporates important geometrical features which ensure maximum stability when full, empty, or inverted, and freedom from milk spillage when tilted. Attention has also been given to good drainage, ease of cleaning and design of a lid which completely protects the can rim and the can contents from contamination. It is mass produced in very large numbers by the dairy engineering industry for both home and export buyers". E.L. Crossley was Professor of Dairying at the University of Reading, England.

Some dairy factories had problems with cans going 'missing'. Presumably the missing cans were used for purposes other than holding milk. One method of addressing this problem was to put a spot of a certain colour of paint on each can received at the dairy over a period of about a week. The colour of the paint spots was changed after a count of the cans.

Empty milk cans scattered across the countryside must have caused some consternation. The New York milk war broke out in 1883, following milk farmers' demands for higher prices. Spilling committees were established and milk was dumped. Occasionally milk strikes and milk wars led to the dumping of milk and scattering of empty milk cans across roads or beside railway lines.

The role of children on dairy farms has been largely overlooked. The following is a brief comment from Canada. "I am so grateful for being raised on a farm until I was 14. On stormy winter days, or if it was raining, the milkman (who picked up our cans of milk at the end of Spruce Lane) would let us five kids pile into the cab of his truck (this was before seatbelts were ever thought of). He dropped us off at Hickson Public School some two miles away, which was near the dairy."

Cynthia Piper in her book '*Billy-can to Carton*' makes several references to children. "Children played an important role in the development of farming in New Zealand. Children who helped milk before school were often up at 4 o'clock in the morning". "One child, Dave Mills, began hand milking cows when he was eight years old. After milking he had a six mile walk to school. He could not play sport after school as he had to go home to milk. Taking the milk to the creamery tended to be a boy's responsibility whereas girls learned to make butter and cheese. Bill and his brothers took the farm milk to the creamery on horseback. They had no need of saddles and the cans were balanced on bags filled with fern fronds".

Boys will be boys. *The Illustrated News* of 1876 reported that a boy put a frog in a milk can, much to the dairy maid's horror when the frog jumped out. Children have been trapped in the large dairy cans leading to the can bottom having to be removed to extract them. One report mentions a toddler drowning in a milk can. Finally, there are a few records of adults and children being injured or killed by dairy cans falling on them.

TRANSPORT: MANUALLY

In the earliest times, cows were taken from door to door and any small vessel would have been used to collect and carry milk or cream. Milk buckets and pails (some with lids) came in many designs and one method of carrying two cans at a time was with a wooden shoulder yoke. Alternatively a can could be carried on the back (a practice that continued well into the twentieth century).

A beautiful drawing from around 1850-57 of a Dutch milkmaid shows how the milk can was supported by a leather knot on her back and held by straps through her shoulders. Another practice that continues today is to carry two milk cans, one at each end of a rod resting on one shoulder.

In an article about *The Retail Milk Trade in London, Circa 1790-1914*, P.J. Atkins writes that in the eighteenth century, vendors had become responsible for the majority of retail milk sales and the 'milkmaids' became part of the folklore of London's streets.

A 1793 engraving by Luigi Schiavonetti (from the series 'Cries of London') depicts a milkmaid with a yoke around her neck and two dairy pails or cans at her feet. She would have almost certainly obtained the milk from cows kept in local buildings within London itself. This method of transporting dairy cans was common in Britain and Western Europe for over 200 years.

Kristine Hughes 1998 book *Everyday Life in Regency and Victorian England (1811-1901)* includes fascinating descriptions of milkmaids at work. The delivery and sale of milk was undertaken entirely by women. Their day began between 4 and 6 a.m. with milking the cows. By 6 p.m. a second delivery had been completed and cans were washed for the next day's work. It was not unusual for milkmaids to walk their animals to houses where milk was drawn straight from the animal to the customer's containers.

Another account (by J. Nelson and quoted by P.J. Atkins) describes the work of milkmaids as an arduous routine. "The milk is conveyed from the cow-house, and sold principally by robust Welsh girls and Irish women: it is amazing to witness the fatigue these females undergo…. They arrive here by 3:00 or 4:00 o'clock in the morning laughing and singing to the music of their empty pails, with these when filled, they return to town: and the weight they are accustomed to carry on their yokes, for several miles, is sometimes from 100-130 lbs".

According to J. Timbs in his 1855 book '*The Curiosities of London – the Dairyman*' the milkmaid had, at the time of writing, disappeared from the streets of London but the yoke and pail as a means of transport continued for a further 30 years.

In the early 1800s, milk was four pence per quart (Atkins, 1980). That was at a time when there were twelve pennies to the shilling and twenty shillings in a pound (or 240 pence to a pound). Also in the early 1800s there were about 8,500 cows in London. Diluting milk with water was common, a problem continued well into the twentieth century. For example, in March 1918, a Mr. John Evans, milk vendor, was fined 20 pounds for adulterating milk. The defense claimed that a large quantity of snow had fallen in to the can. The magistrate did not believe the story.

It seems that milkmen had replaced milkmaids by the late 19th Century. A delightful photograph of a milkman from that time shows him carrying two pails and several small dairy cans. This photograph is from Tom Phelp's informative book '*The British Milkman*' published in 2010 by Shire Publications. The total weight of each full pail or can carried by the milkmaid or milkman would have been at least 14 kg (30.8 lbs). A 'milk carriage' (a large milk can slung on two large carriage wheels) used around 1800 is illustrated in Ward Lock's *Book of Farm Management and Country Life*. Another long established practice was to carry a modified dairy can (similar to a backpack) on their back. This method was used during the early twentieth century.

The use of milk carriages, perambulators (prams) and carts for transporting dairy cans dates back to the late eighteenth century. They were beautifully decorated, some with gold lettering. Milk carts in particular were a major means of delivering milk and were used in their thousands. Both men and boys were employed to deliver milk with the aid of milk prams. For example, in Liverpool, boys worked for Harrison's Waverley Creamery and delivered milk both before and after school.

The London Dairy Supply Co. carts serviced the whole of the London Metropolitan area. It was quoted at the time that the carts travelled 292,000 miles in a year. The milk carts and milk perambulators looked clean but cleanliness was something to be desired as they went from door to door. The same perambulators were later converted to carry bottles.

Hand milk-carts were also the main means of delivering milk around many cities during the early twentieth century. Despite the terrible conditions during WW1, such carts continued to be employed in many cities. The *Illustrated War News* from 1917 shows a steel-helmeted women in Rheims (Northern France) dispensing milk from cans on a hand cart.

In London, around 1877, George Liddiard (cowkeeper) worked from No. 6 Ledbury Mews. Under the Contagious Diseases (Animals) Act of 1869, his premises were declared to be an infected place. A rare photograph (glass plate) taken in the early 1900s shows G. Liddiard's milk tricycle complete with a large delivery can and smaller cans attached.

Both hand barrows and wheel barrows have been made specifically for wheeling milk cans and many modified wheelbarrows have been reported, including one in *Popular Mechanics* (1923, p. 787).

TRANSPORT: DOG CARTS AND HORSE DRAWN CARTS

By the mid-1860s, milkmaids with their yokes were becoming less common and were being replaced by milk carts. For example, in the late nineteenth century and early twentieth century, dog carts were common sights in the larger cities of Europe and the U.S.A. Carts with either two or four wheels were used to transport bread, tea, garden produce, and milk cans. Hand-coloured postcards from the early 1900s of dogs pulling milk carts suggest that in Belgium and the Netherlands this was a major tourist attraction. Such carts were the subject of Delft ware ornaments. Small badges depicting dog carts were also made.

Horse drawn milk carts (and sledges) were common in Britain from about the late nineteenth century. They must have made a beautiful sight with their brightly coloured paintwork and shiny brass and steel cans. Trade catalogues from that time describe their features and list prices.

Milk deliveries from a horse and cart in the early hours led to complaints about the noise. In the 1920s milk carts were fitted with pneumatic tyres. Rubber horseshoes were tried but were not successful.

TRANSPORT: MECHANISED

Cycles, motorcycles, barges, riverboats, lorries (trucks), trains, and public transport were all used to transport milk cans and continue to be used. As late as 1988, an FAO report on village milk processing and transportation refers to 50 litre aluminium cans as suitable for carriage by bicycle. A drawing of a man on a bicycle, complete with a dairy can and bucket is included in the report. Transporting milk cans by bicycles and motor cycles is common in parts of India and Sri Lanka. The diversity of milk cans carried on motorcycles includes some very old, large spherical brass cans while others are modern stainless steel.

Barges laden with milk cans on the canals in England were once a common sight. In Australia, the use of milk boats along the Murray River (from 1919 to 1940's) has been well documented by Ronald Parson in his 1987 book Ships of the inland rivers: an outline history and details of all known paddles ships, barges, and other vessels trading on the Murray-Darling system (published by Gould Books, South Australia). The Mokau River in the North Island of New Zealand has also had a long history of riverboats including those transporting milk cans.

During the years from about 1910 to 1920, Lorries were used to transport milk cans (and other goods) in many parts of the world. The most common size of can was the ten gallon can.

Public transport has and is still used to transport milk cans. In parts of India, a not uncommon sight in the early morning is the transport of milk cans on the sides of public vehicles.

In 1867, there was much debate about the best shape for milk cans being transported by trains. The London *Proceedings of the Journal of the Society of Arts* compared practices in England with that in France. The Great Western Railway was asked about regulations regarding the size and shape of milk cans to which they replied "there were no regulations". It was reported that in France there were special milk trains and that French milk cans were about half the size of those used in England and so therefore easier to handle. The shape of the French cans

allowed them to be packed with great economy of space on both levels of the two floors in the rail vans. It was also noted that the cans had linen coverings which were watered and kept wet.

A common sight on London railway milk-dock platforms in the early 1900s was many hundreds of full milk cans being delivered and empty cans ready for return. The most common were the steel cans or railway churns as they were called. Previously, wooden conical butter churns were used to transport milk but these were found to be too heavy. The conical shape was retained in the galvanised steel versions as they were less likely to topple over. The volume was standardised to 17 gallons and they were easily stacked. The cylindrical design with a mushroom-shaped lid and holding just ten gallons was introduced in the 1930s (see Russ Elliott's commentary 'Conical 17-Gallon Churns' at http://www.gwr.uk/nochurns.html (accessed May 2017).

Railway milk docks were common wherever there were railways. In comparison to the large, bustling, noisy milk docks there were vast numbers of small town milk docks. An image (circa 1910) of a milk dock at the Tongala Railway station in the Goulburn Valley in Australia is one example. Like so many photographs, the shape and size of the milk cans is clearly visible.

The rough treatment of milk cans on the railways was occasionally the subject of criticism. In a Dairy Supply Co. advertising booklet (circa 1880) for 'Barham's Everlasting Steel Churns' there was the following comment: "Owing to the immense wear and tear of milk churns on the English Railways, caused by the bumps of destruction being so largely developed in the heads of Railway Porters, and also to the great advances lately made in the improvement and cheapening of the manufacture of steel, Mr. Barham had had steel plates specially made for the purpose with the most gratifying results".

The following personal observations are extracted from the New Zealand Farmer (1921). "The milk can is a fairly familiar feature on the railway platform, and it very certainly appears to be the object of active hostility. We may well wonder at the ingenuity that is displayed in the handling of these cans, or how to affect the greatest damage in the most innocent of method. An instance of this was witnessed some time ago at a southern railway station. The cans were being transferred from the railway truck across a line of rails at the end of the platform, and at a reasonable distance a heap of metal was convenient. It was observed that the cans were passed from the man on the truck to one on the ground, who dumped them on the steel rail. The rim of the can was assuredly strongly reinforced or there could have been no bottom left to the can, and curiously enough many of them found themselves thrown on the heap of stones, although these stones were not directly in the line of flight, and to the onlooker the milk can failed to appear the appropriate missile for breaking stones. The milk can is not in itself an offensive object, and very assuredly in the empty condition it is far from a laborious task to move it. There are no rough projections that can possibly distress the most delicate hands of even railway employees. As a matter of fact, the milk can has no angles: it is altogether smooth, and provided with well-shaped handles that are all tempting to touch and inviting to the tenderest of lifting and to a setting down of the gentlest. It must be that this very condition of inducement to careful treatment brings about the opposite feeling: "I am helpless and fragile; smash me." There is actually no other way to account for the hostility that is manifested to the milk cans at the railway platform when they are to be moved. It is remarkable that the cans when they are full are to a considerable extent respected and reasonably handled. But the empty cans – pity the owners!

The dairy associations have time and time again approached the Railway Department to secure some amelioration of this milk can damage. This is putting the position mildly; the cans suffer more damage. Every dairyman knows how great is the cost of the wear and tear on the milk cans in ordinary conditions, and how very largely this is increased when they are conveyed on the railway".

The subject of rough treatment of milk cans on the railways prompted a very novel idea. In 1849, a reader of the London Daily News wrote "Instead of the half-churning process of jolting the milk up to London in the luggage vans, why should not the railway companies lay down pipes from the adjacent highland grazing districts and allow the fresh milk to flow by gravity and be drawn off at the metropolitan terminal for retail supply". This was a novel idea akin to that of Heath Robinson's, inventions.

Complaints about the noise created by clanking dairy cans have been common over the years and were not just restricted to horses and cars. Lorries carrying milk cans were also targeted. In 1930, a letter to the U.K. Portsmouth Evening News complained bitterly that the new Traffic Bill does not deal dramatically with one of the worst evils of modern life – noise!

SILENCE THE MILK CHURNS

Sir, - It is a pity that the new Traffic Bill does not deal drastically with one of the worst evils of modern life – noise. Everything possible should be done to silence road vehicles, for the sake of the nation's nerves. I am, in common with my neighbours, frequently wakened at an early hour in the morning by the banging and clanging of a lorry laden with empty milk churns.

If the lorry itself were to run on steel tyres it would not be tolerated for a moment. Solid rubber tyres were bad enough and after they had shaken the foundations of our houses for many a year, they were at least changed for pneumatics when the authorities offered a tax rebate on lorries with air tyres.

Is it not possible to have all milk churns compulsorily fitted with rubber bands?

Hundreds of churns are rattled through hundreds of residential streets every morning and hundreds of people complain about the noise.

When is this daily disturbance going to be stopped? Yours, etc.,

DAVID JAGGER,

30, Oakley Street,

Chelsea, S.W.3.

January 7, 1930.

That letter must have resonated with many people because in the same year, a Derby man invented a device to "kill the clatter". His solution was stout rubber rings that fitted around the churns and acted as a sound cushion. Three years later, the 'silent milk churn' was being promoted by a company of the same name.

UPCYCLING – A NEW LEASE OF LIFE

In some countries, bulk handling of milk has made milk cans obsolete. Not surprisingly the cans went to the scrap metal yards or were forgotten and abandoned in a corner of the farm yard where they slowly rusted away. Recycling, or in this case 'upcycling' is not new. Over the decades many enterprising people have found new or novel uses for old dairy cans and their lids. It was not uncommon for the lids to be used as water bowls or feeding bowls for dogs and poultry. A 1914 British newspaper report was headed 'Churls with Churns" and described alternative uses for churns. "Churns have become bins for storage of seeds and cereals. Some have been taken into the house to be portable pantries and some used for petrol storage" The report goes on to say "to withhold churns is unpatriotic because it operates against one of the most important activities in food distribution. Release your churns and help to secure supplies of our most valuable food!"

Old milk cans are useful containers for almost anything. In 1909 an Australian newspaper reported "Opium in milk cans: The milk can dodge is the latest discovered in connection with the smuggling of opium. The movements of a man carrying milk cans in Australia excited the suspicions of Customs and an investigation revealed 15 tins of opium among the milk". A news report from 1937, was headed "Snakes in Milk Cans – novel use made: the departmental head of Zoology has transported stored snakes (immersed in methylated spirits) from Australia and Papua. The specimens were later transferred to glass jars and displayed for students and visitors."

Such diversity of uses could be good reason for holding a competition for the most novel new uses. In the USA they have proved to be excellent containers for transporting trout for fish re-stocking. In the alpine meadows of Switzerland, groups of upturned dairy cans may have been used as drums. Perhaps intermittent playing on steel drums helps to entertain the lonely life of a shepherd. Alternatively, the cans may have been turned up-side-down to dry after being washed.

New leases of life for dairy cans include letter boxes, planters, floor-standing vases, seats, small tables, flour, bread and seed bins, umbrella stands, soft drink dispensers, kitchen rubbish bins, and even garden rollers. A milk can on its side with wire netting over the mouth was once reported to have been used to restrain a fox. What else? More recent innovative uses include dairy cans in garden water features such as fountains, modern cans converted to lampshades, and in Mongolia some cans have been used as pressure cookers.

Perhaps the most unusual use of a milk can was for a temporary radiator following an accident between a gentleman's vehicle and a traction engine. The vehicle's radiator was destroyed but a makeshift arrangement with a milk can and a piece of garden hose allowed the gentleman to continue for 70 miles to seek help.

MILK CAN ART

Farmyard or folk art using dairy cans could rightly be called 'Dairy Can Art'. This has evolved in many ways through the delights and imagination of practicing arts and crafts. (see for example LL Crafts http://www.crafts.co.uk/milk churns/ accessed February 2018). Entire milk cans have been beautifully painted with various country animals or country scenes – making a warm country welcome to any home. Before painting, some cans have been cut in half so that the height is reduced. Painted cans now grace the entry to homes and some painted cans have been used for advertising or as billboards.

Unfortunately, most examples are unsigned. One of the few exceptions is by Glenys Le Couteur and shows a rooster checking his pocket watch ('Waiting for the Ladies'). Methods for cleaning and decorating old milk cans are described in the appendices.

MILK CANS AND THE ARTS

Milk cans have inspired authors of plays and books. For example, in 1899, a play called *'The Dairy Farm'* by Mrs Archie Cowper (Eleanor Merron) was so popular in New York, with 82 performances, that on the occasion of the 50th performance the management gave away miniature dairy cans.

In a book entitled *'The Milk Can Murder'* by Miles Burton and published in 1935 by Albatross as Vol. 150 in the Albatross Crime Club series, the milk can is the repository for a murder victim.

Photographs of milk cans are very plentiful and indeed it is probable that of all farm yard objects, milk cans are the most photographed. They appear in all kinds of images. During the 1920s and 1930s, there were many Christmas cards and postcards with milk cans as part of the scene. Some cards seemed to dwell on the subject of the miseries suffered after late night drinking. Nevertheless some of those old postcards give useful insights into modes of transport for cans as well as different types of milk cans.

Milk cans have inspired artists. For example the 1825 painting by George Scharf shows a cow keeper's shop in Golden Lane, London. A man is pouring milk from a small container into a milk can made of light coloured metal with brass bands.

Several twentieth century artists have been inspired to paint pictures of milk cans. A 1948 advertisement for the National City Bank in New York included a painting by Clarence Carter called 'Country Milk Run'. This painting not only includes milk cans but also the now rarely seen milk can stand near the farm gate.

Other examples include Mike Garwood in Australia ('Rest-a-while'), in New Zealand Adrienne Pavelka's 'Uncle Fred's Milk can (1985), the Canadian artist's Eleanor McDonald ('Waiting') and Maurice Harvey's painting 'The Dairy Cans' on a plate from the Country Nostalgia Series by W.S. George. The quote on the plate by Maurice Harvey is particularly apt.

> *"Years ago the local dairy thrived, now the rustic charm of*
> *old dairy cans is a reminder of by-gone days."*

Milk cans have inspired people to write poems and there must be no better example than that by Mike Thomas the author of *'Strange Things Happened On My Way to the Zoo'.* The title is *'**Ode to a Greasy Churn'*** and is reproduced with kind permission of the author.

> *O rusty churn, how sad you stand*
> *From Somerset to Samarkaand*
> *We mourn your passing this fair land*
> *Victim of progress and time's hand.*
> *Replaced you are – yet can we thank*
> *The man who thought of the bulk tank?*
> *The farmer's lot, it was his ilk,*
> *To fill you full of foaming milk*
> *But now it is his sorry lot*
> *To fill this plastic tank – this pot*
> *Now, in your place you are discarded,*
> *Flung to some corner – disregarded,*
> *But lo, there's hope.*
> *What is thy plight?*
> *No more to grace us with thy sight*
> *Remember still, you are unique;*
> *In time's small eye you'll be antique –*
> *No longer just an empty hopper;*
> *Thee we immortalise in copper".*

Milk cans have served to save precious documents. Particularly poignant were milk cans used by Warsaw ghetto historian Dr. Emanuel Ringelblum (1900-1944) that helped to preserve the secret "Oneg Shabbat" ghetto archives. A dedicated group of people led by Dr. Ringelblum recorded life in the Ghetto during the Nazi occupation. In 1943, on the eve of the Ghetto's destruction, the archives were placed in three milk cans and metal boxes, then buried in cellars of some buildings. The discovered portion of the archives (about 6,000 documents) are now housed at the Jewish Historical Institute in Warsaw. These archives are the most important collection of documents from the World War II Warsaw Ghetto.

It's not unusual to see milk cans in period dramas. A railway station with cans on a trolley or cans on a stand in the country has often been part of the background or props for a scene.

The ultimate of all artistic endeavours involving milk can must be the work of the land artist Gérard Benoit at the Guillaume (www.bidonssansfrontieres.com). He has constructed many examples of beautiful landscape installations of milk cans. Les Bidons Sans frontières (milk cans without borders or without limits) have appeared across mountains, deserts, snow covered landscapes, and beautiful meadows.

IN THE IMAGE OF THE MILK CAN

The typical milk can shape has inspired designers of many small containers. Early examples included beautiful (silver) pounce pots and mucilage (glue) pots, match holders, and salt and pepper cruets. Around 1900, automaton (musical) milk churns were made in France. They contained a mechanical cat licking its whiskers. In the 1950s there were pencil sharpeners in miniature dairy cans and ceramic containers in the shape of milk cans for storing milk tokens. Modern examples that use the typical milk can shape include confectionary and biscuit containers. Other examples are now sold as garden twine containers or bird feeders. Lampshades have been made out of milk cans for both hanging lamps and standard lamps. In India, beautiful milk can lamps, ideal for siting on desks or tables, have been designed by Sahil and Sarthak (http://www.sahilsarthak.com).

The typical milk can shape has also been adopted by designers of cocktail shakers. A milk can cocktail shaker designed in about 1935 is in the Dallas Museum of Art. This example is silver plate from Reed & Barton. The typical milk can shape

has also been used by architects. Perhaps the largest example is the milk can building in Denver Colorado that houses 'LITLE MAN Ice Cream'. This striking edifice has become a well-known landmark. Elsewhere and in Germany, attractive sales trailers have been designed by ROKA in the shape of a milk cans. Finally, it is disappointing to find that the humble appears to have not to have won the hearts of any museums of art and design.

MINIATURES AND TOY MILK CANS

Some miniature milk cans were made for conferences. For example in 1989, McAnelly Castings in New Zealand made small miniature aluminium cans for he Dominion Milk Vendors Conference in Invercargill. They were used as pen and pencil holders. Miniature milk can ornaments have been produced in great variety. There are for example silver miniature Guernsey milk pots that date from around 1900. Later, W.H. Goss made miniature ceramic Welsh Jack milk cans. In the late 1990s the traditional shape of the English churn was manufactured by Royal Crown Darby. Blue and white models of a milkmaid together with a dog cart holding milk cans have been made in the style of Delft Ware. By way of comparison is the Enid Blyton 'Noddy' model of a milk man with cart and cans. The milk tricycle, milk perambulator, and dog carts have long been made as miniatures. For instance, there is a delightful image of a toy dairy cart in the Army & Navy Stores Catalogue of 1907. More recently twenty-first century manufacturers include Phoenix Miniatures, and the Dutch Company Artitec.

Many toy manufacturers have made not only individual milk cans (such as dolls house miniatures) but also milk trucks loaded with milk cans. In the 1960s Corgi Toys issued a little milk transporter. The Lines Bros. Group made larger Tri-ang tin milk trucks complete with milk churns. Lead railway milk churns have been made and indeed are still made by several model railway manufacturers. It is often said that the Hornby R8678 Skaledale Milk Churns, in particular, suit the 040 Trains N Models.

MILK CAN
GAMES, SPORTS AND ENTERTAINMENT

The famous magician Harry Houdini was well known for his milk can escape, the debut of which took place in 1908 at the Columbia Theatre in St. Louis, U.S.A. The can was specially made for his 'great milk an escape'.

Milk can (churn) street racing has been occurring in Tipperary, Ireland since 1964. A combination of speed and skill is required to control the revolving aluminium churn traveling at speeds up to 40 km per hour. In Asturias, north-west Spain, a similar events have taken place using 35 litre milk churns, except that competitors ran with the cans as far as possible in a given time. The old churns have now been replaced with similarly weighted solid iron cylinders with handles.

In the U.S.A. 'Milk can throw or toss' is one of several fairground games that have been practiced for many years. The object is to toss a softball into a ten gallon milk can from a distance of four to six feet. The game can be made more challenging when the rim of the can is made smaller to be just 1/16th inch large than the softball.

Milk cans have been used to make imitation sports trophies. In 2015 McCaw led the All Blacks in their successful bid to retain the Rugby World Cup. Ritchie McCaw is the most-capped player in rugby union history. McCaw comes from Kurow, a small town in the South Island of New Zealand. There, an imitation 'world cup' trophy made from an upturned gold painted milk can was on prominent display after the successful win.

Milk cans turned into 'cannons' seems would seem an improbable possibility. Not so in the Netherlands during New Year's Eve parties. Take one steel milk can and punch a hole through the wall of the can near the base. Put the can on its side and add a little water then add a lump of calcium carbide. Put the lid on the can and ensure that it fits tightly. Water added to calcium carbide produces the flammable gas acetylene. A flame held to the small hole ignites the gas resulting in an explosion that forces the lid off. It is surely not a game to be recommended.

NOSTALGIA:
SENTIMENTAL YEARNING FOR THE PAST

Yearning for the old days when milk cans were in common use comes in many forms. A series of paintings on plates by W.S. George is called 'country nostalgia' and includes one scene with old milk cans. Another expression of nostalgia has been to restore milk carts and display newly painted old milk cans on railway station trolleys. Replica light-weight cans are made in the image of milk cans and then beautifully decorated as planters and sold at plant nurseries. In some countries such as India, where milk cans continue to be valued and used for transporting milk, decorated replica milk cans are works of art that would not look out of place in any house. Finally, milk cans are readily hired out as props for films and displays.

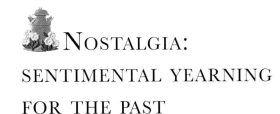

MODERN MILK CANS

Milk cans are still made and continue to be used for transporting milk. In India, several companies manufacture milk cans. These include the Bimal Aluminium PVT Ltd. and Ashish Cans & Containers PVT LTD. Milk cans are also made in China, the USA and Africa. In New Zealand, well known for its dairy industry, milk cans are used for goat herds.

Modern designs for milk cans have been developed. "Global Good, a collaboration between Intellectual Ventures and Bill Gates to invent technology that improves life in developing countries, developed the Milking and Transport System for Kenya after Gates visited an EADD cooperative in 2009". The outcome was the **Mazzi**, a plastic 10 litre container specially designed for carrying milk in under-developed places. www.fastcompany.com/3038785/a-new-milk-can-for-the-developing-world-fun... (accessed 9/7/2018). A modern design for a milk can - surely that is worth celebrating!

THE JOURNEY NOW MOVES FROM TEXT TO IMAGES

▲ *An aerial cable for carrying milk cans. From Popular Mechanics, November 1913.*

PART TWO
A COMPENDIUM OF
MILK CAN IMAGES

HISTORY AND DESIGN

◀ *J. Haydon's Dairy, London. Milk Perambulator.*
Circa 1900. The boy is standing in the perambulator. Courtesy London Borough
of Lewisham.

1,000 YEARS OF HISTORY
GUERNSEY MILK CANS

Guernsey is one of the Channel Islands situated about 30 miles from the Normandy coast of France and 80 miles from England. There, the Guernsey cans have been made by local craftsmen for over 1,000 years and are a relic of Guernsey's Norman ancestry. The cans came over with the original Guernsey cattle in about 980 A.D. The round shape of the cans is strong and is less prone to 'slopping'. The cans had a dual purpose, for transporting milk or cream from the dairy and for serving it at the table. The larger examples were transported on a hand cart, donkey cart or ox cart to the door and measured out into a small can for the table. The standard Guernsey measure was a pot (equivalent to about four pints) and the largest size was five gallons. Originally made from tinned steel plate, copper has been used since the 1870's. The cans are tinned on the inside. The six copper examples shown here range in volume from one gallon (two pots) to 1/8th of a pint. Similar cans are made on the Island of Jersey but are not so common. Refer to the *'oldcopper.org'* website for more details.

ANCIENT INDIAN BRASS MILK POTS

These two traditional containers (right) are of an ancient design and were used in rural villages in India to transport milk or water. Women could carry two or three pots at a time on their head. The cans had tremendous sentimental value and were passed from one generation to another. They are tinned on the inside. The smaller one is approximately seven inches (17.7 cm.) tall. Sadly, they are slowly being replaced by plastic and aluminium cans.

Image of the milk pots courtesy of Sahil Bagga.

Above: Image of women carrying pots on their heads from 'Why do women carry things on their heads?' by Jane Whittle. This is part of the University of Exeter 'Women's work in Rural England, 1500-1700' project.

FROM THE OLD MASTERS

The example of the four gallon brass Dutch milk can (top right) is a rare survivor from the 18th Century.

Below Left. Jan Havicksz Steen (circa 1625-1679). Section of 'Adoration of the Shepherds'. Jan Steen was a Dutch painter and his works are known for their abundant colour and sense of humour. This painting is in the collection of the Rijksmuseum. Amsterdam. The milk can is made of brass, oval shaped and has a tall neck. The lid lies on the floor. The design of this large milk can is typical of the seventeenth and eighteenth centuries in Western Europe.

Below Right. Copy after Aelbert Cuyp (1620-1691) 'A study of milk cans, cows and a milkmaid'. Courtesy of The Morgan Library and Museum, N.Y. Note the use of a funnel and the presence of a yoke lying on the ground.

FROM A SOCIAL CHRONICLER

George Scharf (1820-1895) **'Milk Maids'.** George Scharf was born in London. He was a 'social chronicler of early Victorian London and the pictorial equivalent of Charles Dickens'. This painting shows milkmaids and a milk vendor preparing to sell milk. The vendor is using a tin dipper to decant milk from cylindrical milk cans (with brass rims) into a small brass milk jug. The two milkmaids on the right are exchanging news before they put a wooden yoke around their neck in order to carry two milk cans. The volume of the cans appears to be no more than five gallons each. The total weight for two five gallon cans filled with milk would be about 103lbs. (47 kgs).

Image from an unattributed picture on card.

FROM A FRENCH OLD MASTER

Jean-Francois Millet (1814-1875) 'Study of a woman pouring water into milk cans.' Millet was a French painter noted for his scenes of peasant farmers. This work is in the collection of the Museum of Fine Arts, Boston. Gift of Martin Brimmer. The women has milked the cow (or cows) and is now pouring milk from the wooden pail into two brass milk cans. This design of milk can had no lids and were typical of Normandy, France.

THE ENGLISH DAIRY FARMER

Modern Milk Transport in 1800. A water colour by James Ward. This image is from G.E. Fussell's 1966 book *'The Dairy English Farmer 1500-1900'* published by Frank Cass & Co., Ltd., London. Fussell labelled the image "modern milk transport in 1800". The can would probably hold about six gallons). When the can was full it would need to be counterweighted on the other side of the animal (a pony?). Certain breeds of the domestic donkey (such as the Cotentin Donkey) were used as pack animals, mainly for carrying milk.

DESIGN OF A 'TYPICAL' MILK CAN

This patent was taken out by Henry Wehrhahn of New York in December 1905. The text reads "My invention relates to milk-cans and has for its object to provide means for protecting the can from injury and wear and for making the joints formed in the body of the can as nearly as homogeneous as possible". This could rightly be called a 'typical' milk can design.

Figure 1 is a side elevation.

Figure 2 is a vertical cross section.
A. The body of the can.
B. Bottom of the can.
C. Hoop arranged around the outer wall.
D. Breast of the can.
E. Annular hoop.
F. Handles.
G. Straps for handles.

MILK CAN

No. 808,326.

H. WEHRHAHN.
MILK CAN.
APPLICATION FILED MAR. 7 1905.

PATENTED DEC. 26, 1905.

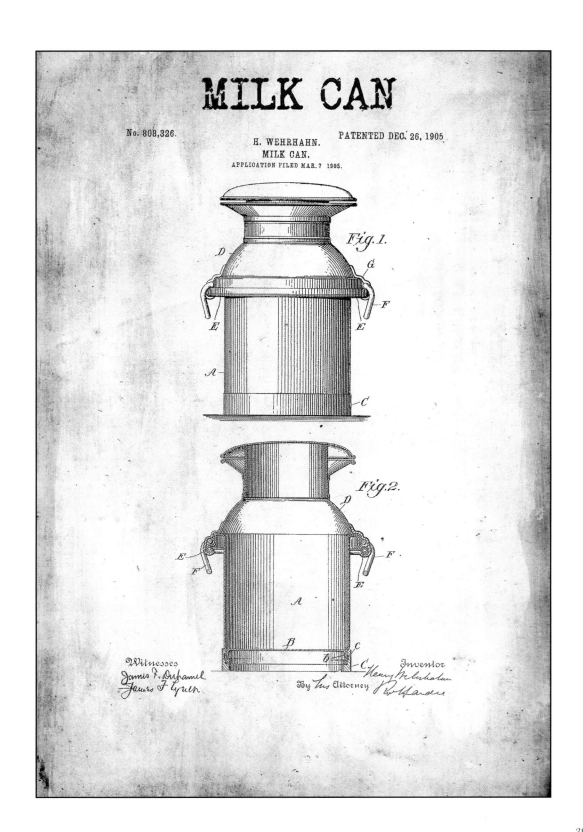

Witnesses
James F. Duhamel
James F. Lynch

Inventor
Henry Wehrhahn
By his Attorney

SPECIALIST HANDLES

Milk can handles are tremendously varied as shown by these few examples.

Above: from Willard's *Practical Dairy Husbandry*. 2nd Edition, 1872.

Right: from top left to bottom right: French ten gallon can for grain or milk; Indian 10-11 gallon reinforced can; New Zealand ten gallon tin can, The Co-op Dairy of Otago Ltd., Dunedin; New Zealand 12-14 steel gallon can with a lid that sits on the inside. Note the brass badge wired to the handle. On one side it says 'The Co-op Dairy of Otago Ltd., Dunedin' and on the other side 'Barry's Bay Co-op, Christchurch, X8'.

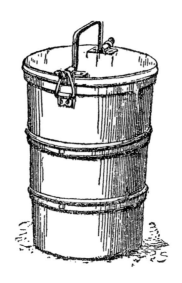

DESIGN SPECIALS

Above is an extension milk pail as advertised in the *New Zealand Farmer* in 1903. The can was designed by a dairyman in the State of New York. The upper end of each section was formed to overlap the bottom of the section above.

Right above: a calf feeding milk can from France (eight inches (20.5 cm) tall excluding the handle).

On the near right is a seven gallon back-pack tin milk can that weighs 22.7 kg (50 lbs) when full. On the far right is a cream setting can. This design dates from about 1879.

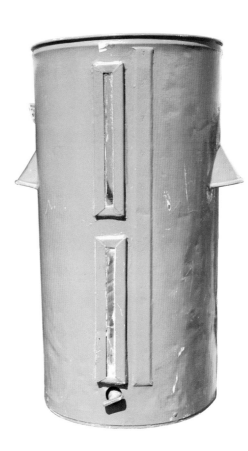

HOMEMADE SPECIALS

On the left is a two gallon 'billy can' with A 339 painted on the side. On the right is a five pint billy can. A hasp and staple and also a hinge have been added. It is inscribed: Empty. Avon Dairy Co. Full. J.T. Norton Lyttelton. The port and town of Lyttleton is near Christchurch, New Zealand.

A CHURN MAKING SHOP

These images are from a 1928 booklet entitled 'A *Look Through a Modern Dairy*'. It shows the Park Royal works of London of the Dairy Supply Co. Ltd.

Images provided by Bob Malcolm.

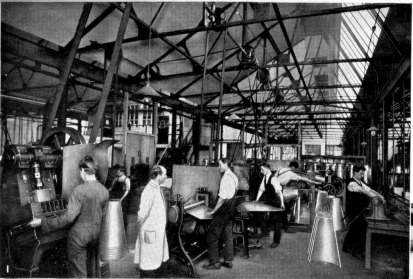

1.—CHURN MAKING SHOP
No. 1, PARK ROYAL
WORKS.

2.—CHURN MAKING SHOP
No. 2, PARK ROYAL
WORKS.

Manufacture of welded milk cans

Photographs of milk cans being manufactured are rare. Above: The body of the can is having the bottle-neck made by spinning. Below: The bottom of the can being electrically welded by a seam welder.

Images from the article Manufacture of welded milk cans by S.F. Crewther (he was attached to Hardleys, Auckland), in *New Zealand Engineering*, pp 113-114, 1953.

THE COW KEEPER

This is another painting by George Scharf. It's at the British Museum and is thought to date from 1825. The location of the Cow Keeper's premises is thought to be in Golden Lane in the City of London. It shows cows in a well- ventilated stall, a window display, a maid serving at the counter, hay being pulled down into the cellar and the cow keeper pouring milk from a small container into a larger milk can which has two brass bands and a handle.

Image from an unattributed picture on card.

THE DAIRY SUPPLY COMPANY'S NEW PREMISES, BLOOMSBURY.

An historic place not to miss

The magnificent photograph on the right (Courtesy of PizzaExpress) is undated but may have been taken in about 1890 when the Dairy Supply Company was fully operational and shows several horse-drawn milk carts and about 60 milk churns.

The building is much the same now as it was in the nineteenth century. The external features remain largely untouched. Now occupied by PizzaExpress (since 1967), the building is a place not to be missed by milk can historians or milk can collectors. Inside PizzaExpress are the original tiles.

Above is a drawing of The Dairy Supply Company's new premises in London in 1889. The entrance was in Duke Street (the street name was changed in 1894 to Coptic Street). The carts entered through a passage from Little Russell Street. The upper portion of the building had numerous suites of dwelling-rooms for the employees.

BEAUTIFUL MATERIALS FOR MILK COUNTER PANS AND OTHER DAIRY REQUISITES

W.T. Copeland & Sons (England) were manufacturers of some of the most beautiful dairy requisites such as counter pans (centre of the image), milk cans with cane handles (left centre), milk pans, and novelty items.

This image is from Copeland's catalogue of 1902 and is reproduced here with kind permission of the Spode Museum Trust.

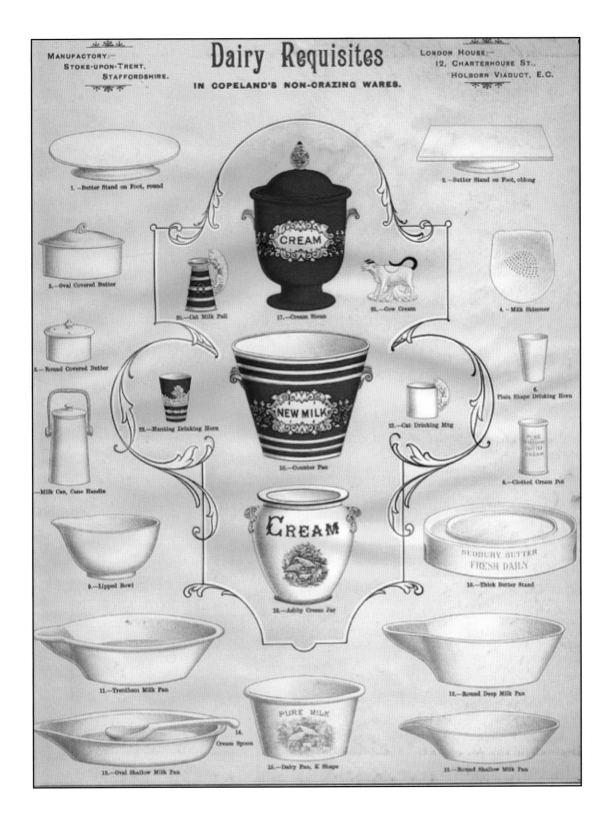

MANUFACTORY:—
STOKE-UPON-TRENT,
STAFFORDSHIRE.

Dairy Requisites

IN COPELAND'S NON-CRAZING WARES.

LONDON HOUSE:—
12, CHARTERHOUSE ST.,
HOLBORN VIADUCT, E.C.

1.—Butter Stand on Foot, round

2.—Butter Stand on Foot, oblong

3.—Oval Covered Butter

20.—Oak Milk Pail

17.—Cream Steen

21.—Cow Cream

4.—Milk Skimmer

6.—Round Covered Butter

23.—Hunting Drinking Horn

NEW MILK

22.—Cat Drinking Mug

16.—Cucumber Pan

6.
Plain Shape Drinking Horn

5.—Clotted Cream Pot

—Milk Can, Cane Handle

9.—Lipped Bowl

CREAM

19.—Ashby Cream Jar

SUDBURY BUTTER
FRESH DAILY

18.—Thick Butter Stand

11.—Trentham Milk Pan

12.—Round Deep Milk Pan

14.
Cream Spoon

PURE MILK

15.—Dairy Pan, K Shape

13.—Oval Shallow Milk Pan

10.—Round Shallow Milk Pan

THE BEST CHINA

China counter pans were introduced in the late nineteenth century. By 1896, the Dairy Supply Co. London, was advertising a beautiful range of novel designs. They ranged in size from four to 24 quarts. The example above (circa 1910) holds two gallons (eight quarts) and is 13 inches tall (33 cm.) and nine inches (23 cm.) wide at the top. The lid has a hinge set near the back and there is an air filter.

COUNTER PANS.

CHINA.—New Oval Design, 1896.

REGISTERED DESIGN SOLD ONLY BY THE DAIRY SUPPLY Co., Ltd.

Since the first China Counter Pan was introduced by us some years ago, it has never been improved upon.

We are now able to offer a Pan, not only novel in design, but much in advance as regards appearance. It is oval in shape, made in Faience ware of the very highest class, and of the same style as is very popular for general use. The centre of the front of the Pan is formed in a panel, coloured in shades of blue, green, or brown; across this panel runs a spray of Wild Roses, slightly raised and in natural colours. The words "Pure Milk" appear clearly on a ribbon above this panel.

The design, material, and workmanship all add to the cost of this extremely pretty pan, but by making special arrangements at the Potteries and ordering a large number we are able to offer at the same price as the old patterns.

In one size only to hold 16 quarts   ..   ..   ..   £2 5s.

A stock is always kept of pans with Wild Roses on blue, green, or brown panels. Other flowers, such as Marguerites or Chrysanthemums on panels of the above colours are sometimes in stock, and can always be made to order.

ORIGINAL ROUND DESIGN.

First introduced by the Dairy Supply Company, Limited, and since extensively copied. Made in two patterns, "The Hooped" and "Fluted."

In three styles—Marone and Gold, Blue and Gold, or Green and Gold, with "New Milk" or "Separated Milk" in Gold Letters.

	£	s.	d.
20 quarts	2	5	0
12 "	1	7	6

Pure White and Black Letters.

	s.	d.
20 quarts	18	0
10 "	12	6

The "Fluted" is made in 20 quart size only.

Hooped Pattern.

Fluted Pattern.

WHITE CHINA MILK PANS.

With "New Milk" in Black Letters.

	s.	d.		s.	d.
To hold 4 quarts	2	0	To hold 13 quarts	7	0
" 5 "	2	6	" 18 "	8	6
" 6 "	3	3	" 20 "	10	6
" 8 "	4	0	" 24 "	12	6
" 10 "	5	0			

Very cheap and strong, easily cleaned, and are the best Counter Pans, suitable for small Dairies.

TIN COUNTER PANS.

Brass Hoops top and bottom, and Brass Handles.

	s.	d.		s.	d.
8 quarts	8	0	16 quarts	13	6
10 "	10	0	20 "	15	6
12 "	11	0	30 " £1	2	0
14 "	13	0			

Solid Brass Handles, as shown, of handsome design, 3/6 extra. Engraved Plate for front extra, according to design and size.

SPECIAL COUNTER PANS made to Order, in copper, brass, or nickel, designs submitted.

A taste of India

These three brass come from India. They are tinned on the inside. Thought to be milk cans, they hold one, two and six pints respectively. The two pint can has the initials G.S.V. All have the same basic decoration of engine turned parallel lines. They are 'solid' cans with hinged lids and a hasp and staple so that padlocks can be applied.

COPPER MILK CANS

Above: a one gallon copper can from South Africa with a badge (TSP) and the inscriptions A.W.C. Green Point.

Left: Carnation Milk five gallon copper milk can. Carnation evaporated milk was established in the USA in 1899.

Right: Cadbury Bros. Ltd., (England) eight gallon copper milk can with gallon marks indented on one side. The letter 'M' and number '13965' appears on the neck of the can.

Both cans probably date from the 1930s and were possibly limited editions. They are not tinned on the inside. The handles on these two cans are different, as are the lids.

61

Materials and designs
for a world of metal milk cans

Above: a 1976 25 L milk can from Russia.

Next page from top left to bottom right: a 15 litre copper can from Argentina with the inscription TAMBO LA VACA LIJAN ANO 19231 LM; a Dutch enamelled 'melk can' of four pints; an aluminium 1.5 litre can from Portugal with the inscription 'Feito-em-Portugal'; a three litre steel can from Slovakia; a French 20 litre Aluminium can with the letters and words ILCO Schmid protex Marque & Modeledeposes; a two gallon tin can from the U..S.A. with the inscription Arden Farms Co. 9 Reg. Cal. 59.

From the Dairy Supply Company, London 1880 - 1881

Many different designs were made for specific uses. There were hand cans (½ gill - six quarts), bottles (one pint 30 quarts), kettles (six quarts - 14 quarts), and carriers' pails (12 quarts 20 quarts). The hand cans fitted on milk perambulators. It is not known what the bottles were used for. The kettles had a bracket on each side to hold hand cans.

KETTLES.

Of best double-tinned Steel.

	With Brass Hinges, and Hoops for hanging Cans.		Brass Mounted, with Bands top and bottom.		Inside Rims, to prevent spilling. Extra.	
	s.	d.	s.	d.	s.	d.
6 Quarts	6	0 ..	8	0	1	0
8 ,, ...	7	0 ..	9	6	1	0
10 ,, ...	9	0 ..	11	0	1	6
12 ,, ...	10	6 ..	11	6	1	6
14 ,, ...	11	6 ..	13	0	1	6

Engraved Brass Covers, from 3/6 extra.

CARRIERS' PAILS.

Brass Hoops, Hinges, and Bands for Smaller Cans. Covers ornamented with Brass.

12 Quarts (each Pail) per pair	.. ..	£1 7 0
16 ,, ,, ,,	.. ..	1 12 0
20 ,, ,, ,,	.. ..	1 16 0

Name Stamped in Body or Lid free of charge.

Engraved Plates for the Covers	.. ..	3s. per pair extra.
,, ,, Bodies	.. ..	5s. ,,

[TAP PAILS MADE TO ORDER.

YOKES AND STRAPS.

For carrying the above.

Plain Yoke, Mounted with Brass, from ..	.. ..	5 6 each
Painted with Gold Letters	.. ..	12 0 ,,
Straps..	.. ..	8 0 per pair
Brass Hooks	.. ..	1 9 ,,
Yokes and Chains, complete	.. ..	5 6 each.

UNIFORMS.

MILKMEN'S JACKETS.

Size round chest in inches—	34	35	36	37	38	39	40	42
White Twill	4s. 6d.,	4s. 9d.,	5s.,	5s. 3d.,	5s. 6d.,	5s. 9d.,	6s.	6s. 3d.
Drill, best	5s. 3d.,	5s. 9d.,	6s.,	6s. 3d.,	6s. 9d.,	7s. 3d.,	7s. 6d.,	7s. 9d.

Blue Collars and Cuffs no extra charge. Half-inch Blue Letters on Collars, 1½d. per letter.

BLUE SERGE APRONS, 2s. 3d., 2s. 6d., 2s. 9d. each.

STERILIZING APPARATUS.

The process of sterilizing milk has found great favour in Continental Dairies, where it may be said to be in general use. It requires glass bottles to contain the milk, and which are air-tight when closed, and also a boiler heated by steam or a fire to raising the temperature of the bottled milk, sufficiently high to kill all the bacteria in the milk.

In modern times of bacteria and fear on the part of many of diseases being spread by milk, there is no doubt a good field for the supply of sterilized milk as a special article, particularly for infants. Milk which has been sterilized is free from all chance of infection, and will keep any length of time before it is opened.

Bottles with air-tight stoppers, to hold ½-pint ..	.. .. ..	£2 12s. per hundred
,, ,, ,, ,, 1 pint almost..	.. ..	£3 ,,

Boilers, heated by steam or fire, according to requirements, of size and situation.

By the hand

Many of these oval hand cans from London dairies have survived and are very collectable, particularly if they are labelled with the name of the dairy. This group of seven are all tinned steel with lovely brass fittings. They include an eight pint can, a quart can (letter 'O' on the base), two different shapes of the one pint can (one with '1' on the bottom), a one pint can from the Dairy Supply Co., a half pint, a quarter pint or gill (Welford & Sons London) and the tiny 1/8th of a pint or half a gill.

LARGE AND VERY LARGE

These two examples are the largest of all the milk cans that could be manoeuvred by one or two persons. On the right is a splendid example of a galvanised delivery milk can that was transported on a milk perambulator. It holds 17 gallons (marked on the side), has a tap on the bottom, a lockable lid and an air vent. It is inscribed Monkton Farm Dairy, Birchington (in Kent, England). The example above is a 24 gallon galvanised milk can inscribed Wilkins Limited Dairy Plant Works Invercargill (New Zealand). It has a riveted seam on the side and a pair of hinged handles. The lid fits neatly into the can.

LIKE RUSSIAN NESTED DOLLS

The 'typical' steel milk can from the early to mid-twentieth century was made in many different sizes (height and diameter at the base are given in cm.). The examples shown here are one gallon (27x19cm.), two gallons (35x22.5cm.), four gallons (43x28 cm.), six gallons (50x31.5 cm.), eight gallons (58.5x37 cm.) and ten gallons (67x38 cm.). The last had the lid replaced, possibly because it was lost or damaged. Lids were often made specifically for each milk can and would fit neatly into that can only. Note the 'location' numbers on some of the cans and the brass badges that give both the farm name and the dairy name. The four gallon can (from New Zealand) has a luggage label attached (a rare survivor) that reads: "From Tai Tapu Fernleaf Butter Factory Christchurch. Z-18".

RARE AND UNCOMMON

The ten gallon steel milk can on the left has several unusual design features. It has straight sides, a lid with a brim that fits over the can, a brass tightening device for the lid (see above), and heavy brass handles. It was made by a manufacturer in Christchurch, New Zealand. The firm of 'Adcock' were local tinsmiths and sheet metal workers and was established by E.J. Adcock in 1887. The firm was in existence until 1983 when Graeme Adcock was the last manager. A locally made milk can with such unusual design features is very rare.

The 12 gallon aluminium can on the right is painted green and is stamped with three crowns. This suggests it was a military milk can. These are relatively uncommon survivor compared to farm milk cans.

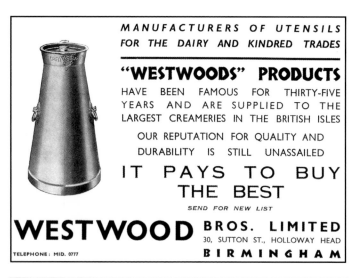

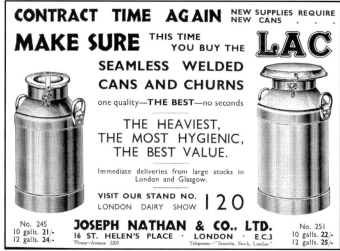

SEAMLESS CANS

By the 1930's, many can manufacturers were making seamless cans. These are a few of the advertisements from 1933.

Images provided by Bob Malcolm.

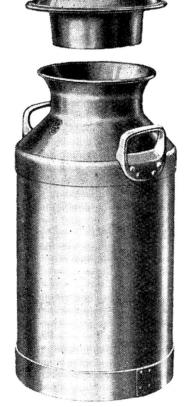

IDEAL FOR GRUELLING HARD WARE

In the 1920s, Alex Harvey & Sons Ltd. made 'seamless' milk cans. These ranged in size from 12 to 25 gallons. Their widespread newspaper advertisements showed graphic scenes of empty cans being treated with less care than might be desired. Alex Harvey were based in Auckland, New Zealand and were well known for the "RV" and "IDEAL" brands of milk cans. The "RV" may have been an abbreviation of "harvey".

THE IDEAL SEAMLESS FACTORY MILK CAN

BY FAR THE CLEANEST, STRONGEST AND MOST DURABLE CAN ON THE MARKET.   ENTIRELY SEAMLESS.

NO RIVETED OR SOLDERED SEAMS.

SEAMLESS LID.

SPECIAL SECTION TOP HOOP.

CENTRE HOOP FITTED WITH UNBREAKABLE HANDLES.

Being absolutely seamless all dirt and germs are assiduously and unfailingly repelled.

The insides being of a smoothness comparable with the surface of glass, no habitation is afforded for particles of even the most minute nature.

Made out of material with special tinning qualities. Special care is exercised in the tinning process. Each can is tinned four times with pure tin, leaving an extra heavy coating of tin.

On page four you will see Sectional View of the IDEAL Can showing details of construction.

Capacity:	25 Gall.	20 Gall.	16 Gall.	12 Gall.
PRICE:	84/-	72/6	69/-	62/6.

THE LAST OF THE FARM MILK CANS

By the 1950s the last of the milk cans were being used on dairy farms. This image shows four large galvanised steel cans (15-25 gallons) that were last used on a farm in the North Island of New Zealand by an Indian family. The number '133' denotes the milk can supplier. The 25 gallon can stood 133 inches (77.5 cm.) high and 19 inches (47.5 cm.) wide. The cans were made by Hardleys, Auckland.

MILK TANKS

This image shows a milkmaid in the Netherlands on her morning round. Taken about 1904, she is pushing a milk tank on a very solid wooden cart that was probably made specifically for the milk tank. Larger milk tanks, on horse-drawn carts, were not uncommon in some other European countries.

Image from a stereoscope slide, 'From *Notes of Travel No. 22*, copyright 1905 by Underwood and Underwood.

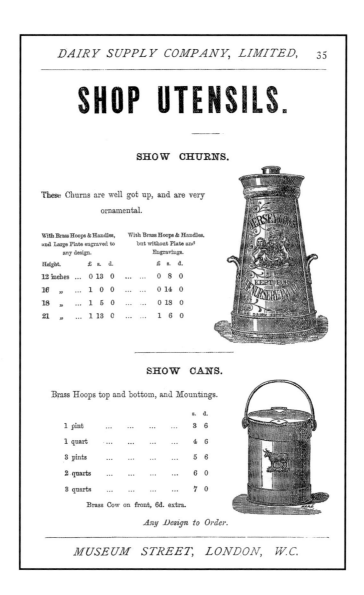

SHOP UTENSILS.

SHOW CHURNS.

These Churns are well got up, and are very ornamental.

	With Brass Hoops & Handles, and Large Plate engraved to any design.		With Brass Hoops & Handles, but without Plate and Engravings.	
Height.	£	s.	d.	£	s.	d.
12 inches	0	13	0	0	8	0
16 „	1	0	0	0	14	0
18 „	1	5	0	0	18	0
21 „	1	13	0	1	6	0

SHOW CANS.

Brass Hoops top and bottom, and Mountings.

					s.	d.
1 pint	...	...	...	...	3	6
1 quart	...	...	...	...	4	6
3 pints	...	...	...	...	5	6
2 quarts	...	...	...	...	6	0
3 quarts	...	...	...	...	7	0

Brass Cow on front, 6d. extra.

Any Design to Order.

MUSEUM STREET, LONDON, W.C.

CHURNS ON SHOW

Ornamental metal churns and cans were used for dairy window displays. Catalogues from the London Dairy Supply Co. London, in the 1880s illustrate several examples. These are now exceedingly rare and perhaps that is a reason why the example on the right is a modern reproduction. About ten years ago these 'Skidmore' brass cans were copied and made in three sizes, possibly in India or China. This example is 20 inches (52 cm.) high.

A RARE GLIMPSE OF
A DECORATIVE MILK CHURN ON SHOW

Pottery show churns were beautifully decorated and would have been made by most of the well-known Staffordshire potteries such as Wedgwood, Copeland and Spode. In this evocative photograph, two pottery show churn can be seen on either side of the shop window. A metal milk can stands outside.

From p. 213 of *Lost London: 1870-1945* by Phillip Davies and published in 2009 by Transatlantic Press - an English Heritage photograph)

The rare example on the right is a small decorative shop display churn Pure Country Milk depicting a dairymaid and a cow. It is stamped with the Dairy Supply Co. logo on the base.

The image was kindly provided by The Antique Dispensary Ltd., England.

AMERICAN HISTORY – MILK CANS FROM HOME AND COMMUNITY LIFE (1875-1900)

These six small milk cans are in the National Museum of American History, Kenneth E. Behring Centre. Their small size and simplicity contrast with the large 8-10 gallon steel cans. From top left to bottom right. Two-quart milk can made in five pieces, two-quart milk can with a low-domed cover made in four pieces, two-quart milk can made in four pieces with a brass tag stamped 'C. Jewett', three-quart milk can made in four pieces with a brass tag stamped 'F. Fuller', a one-quart milk can made in four pieces with a low-domed cover and a cast letter 'S', a two-pint milk can made in four pieces.

WELSH JACKS OR ST. DAVID'S CANS?

These two simple-shaped tin cans came from Wales (U.K). The one on the left holds two imperial pints and that on the right holds twelve Imperial pints. The similar shaped Goss Ware miniature above (4 inches, 10.2 cm.) has the base mark 'model of a Welsh Jack'. It is curious that this 'model' promotes Margate in Kent (England) rather than Wales (U.K.). The origin of the term 'Welsh Jack' is unknown. Are the two cans 'Welsh Milk Jacks'?

Alternatively are these two cans St. David's cans? A reference to 'St. David's can' was made in 1977 in an article on "Bygones from the Dairy' in the magazine *Art & Antiques*". A photograph was not included. The author describes these cans as "the favourite utensil of the Welsh dairies and that they are rarely seen today. No other information can be found apart from the passing reference by Sonia Roberts in the 1977 issue of *Art and Antiques*.

MILK IN SQUARE CANS FOR THE LINERS

Taken in 1961 at Southampton (England) these two photographs shows small square cans being filled with milk for P.& O. Orient Lines Ship. The merger of P.& O. with Orient Lines took place in 1960. The milk cans were this size and shape for ease of handling and storage on board ship.

Photographs supplied by Bob Malcolm.

PROMOTING AND
ADVERTISING MILK CANS

OK-3288

TRADE CATALOGUES

This page is from a Charles Williams Store Catalogue dated 1913. The Charles William Stores in New York City were a very successful retail chain and mail order house during the 'roaring twenties'. The variety of milk cans is as impressive as the names of the cans.

ELGIN CAN

No. 27B7001

The Elgin Pattern Milk Can is the favorite in the dairy districts of Illinois, and its use is spreading throughout the country. This can is made of heavier metal than the Iowa, especially in the 10-gallon size. The bottom hoop is inside the flange and supports the bottom.

Size, 5 Gal.; approximate shipping wt., 11½ lbs. Price, each, **$1.65**

Size, 8 Gal.; approximate shipping wt., 18 lbs. Price, each, **$2.10**

Size, 10 Gal.; approximate shipping wt., 21½ lbs. Price, each, **$2.37**

WILLIAMS SPECIAL CAN

No. 27B7005

The Williams Special Milk Can is made 3 inches taller and somewhat smaller in diameter than the standard 8-gal. can so three will fit abreast in the standard wagon box. This can has the famous Williams bottom with curved malleable iron breast handles and special reinforcing hoop where the breast is joined to body.

Size, 8 Gal.; approximate shipping wt. 19½ lbs. Price, each, **$2.34**

SPECIAL DELIVERY CAN

No. 27B7014

The Williams Special Delivery Can enables one man to carry a 5-gallon can in each hand instead of two men carrying one 10-gallon can. While this can is largely used in dairies, it is also used for delivering oil or any kind of liquid.

Size, 5 Gal.; approximate shipping wt., 11 lbs. Price, each **$1.86**

WILLIAMS CAN

No. 27B7010 The Williams Pattern Can is widely used. The construction is shown by the picture. You will notice that no rivets are used in fastening the bottom, and from the way it is made, it is impossible for the bottom to come off.

Size, 5 Gal.; approximate shipping wt., 11¾ lbs. Price, each, **$1.74**

Size, 8 Gal.; approximate shipping wt., 18½ lbs. Price, each, **$2.16**

Size, 10 Gal.; approximate shipping wt., 22 lbs. Price, each, **$2.49**

MILK CAN LINKS AND WASHERS

No. 27B7040 Are used for attaching cover to the milk can.

Price, attached to can, each.. **5c**

COPPER MILK CAN LETTERS

No. 27B7045

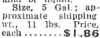

We solder any number of letters or figures you desire on any milk can that you purchase. Size, 1⅝ inches. Price, per letter or figure put on can, each.............. **1½c**

MOHAWK CAN

No. 27B7002

Our Mohawk Pattern Can has the famous Williams bottom and extra heavy umbrella cover. New style curved malleable iron handles with bar plate on the breast, which is a distinct advantage. This style can is largely used in all sections of the East.

Size, 8 Gal.; size of neck, 6⅛ in.; approximate shipping weight, 19½ lbs. Price, each **$2.46**

Size, 10 Gal.; size of neck, 7¼ in.; approximate shipping weight, 26½ lbs. Price, each.................. **$2.82**

NEW YORK CAN

No. 27B7011

Our New York Pattern Milk Can is used extensively throughout the East and is sold to some customers in the Western States. Is furnished with our umbrella top cover and curved drop handles. The inside bottom hoop is thoroughly tinned.

Size, 5 Gal.; size of neck, 6⅛ in.; approximate shipping weight, 15½ lbs. Price, each, **$1.86**

Size, 10 Gal.; size of neck, 7¼ in.; approximate shipping wt., 26½ lbs. Price, each........ .... **$2.75**

GREEN MOUNTAIN MILK CAN.

No. 27B7015

Our Green Mountain Pattern Milk Can is the same as our New York style in construction, but lighter material is used in the 10-gal. size and it weighs between 4 and 5 pounds less.

Size, 5 Gal.; approximate shipping weight, 15½ pounds. Price, each, **$1.86**

Size, 10 Gal.; approximate shipping weight, 22 lbs. Price, each.. **$2.55**

TRADE CATALOGUES

This 1917 example is from a former leading hardware specialist based in Chicago called Hibbard, Spencer, Bartlett & Co. The sizes range from 40 gallons to the small two gallons. The patterns are as diverse as are the capacities of the milk cans.

MILK CANS.

ELGIN PATTERN.

COMPETITION.

All Tubular Handles, Regular Pattern Cover, Seamless One Piece Bowl and Neck, Seamless Breast, Strong Breast Hoops, Bottom Hoop Inside with Flush Flange at Bottom on Which Body and Bottom Rest, all Retinned.

Nos.	105	108	110
Capacity, gal..	5	8	10
W't each, lbs..	12	14	17
Per dozen	$23.00	26.00	28.00
	BAJJ	BCDJ	BEBJ

A good general purpose can.

IOWA PATTERN.

EXTRA QUALITY COMPETITION.

All Tubular Handles, Regular Pattern One Piece Cover, Seamless One Piece Bowl and Neck, Seamless Breast, Stout Breast Hoop and Strong Outside Bottom Hoop, Extra Well Made and Retinned for a Can in this Grade.

Nos.	205	208	210
Capacity, gal..	5	8	10
W't each, lbs..	12	15	17
Per dozen	$24.00	27.00	29.00
	BABE	BDFJ	BFEJ

Special No. 608—8 gal. heavy Iowa,, malleable handles, per doz. BHBJ $47.00

EXTRA HEAVY.

7¼ Inch Neck, Seamless Bottom and Body, Seamless Breast, Sanitary One Piece Cover, Malleable Handles.

Nos.	532	540
Capacity, gal.	8	10
W't each, lbs.	19	21
Per dozen	$56.00	60.00
	CCFJ	CFJJ

ELGIN PATTERN. EXTRA QUALITY.

THE BEST IN CANS.

Heavy all Tubular Handles, Regular Pattern, Seamless Covers, Heaviest Welded Breast and Bottom Hoops, Bottom Hoops Have Flange Flush With Outside of Can—Except No. 305—on Which Bottom and Sides Rest, all Thoroughly Well Retinned and Soldered.

For General Purpose, Medium Weight.

Nos.	305	308	310
Capacity, gal..	5	8	10
W't each, lbs..	12	15	17
Per dozen	$25.00	28.00	30.00
	AEJJ	AFHJ	AHJJ

Heavy Hard Service Can.

Nos.	408	410
Capacity, gal..	8	10
W't each, lbs.	19	20
Per dozen	$30.00	33.00
	AHJJ	AIJJ

Extra Heavy R. R. Shipping Can.

Nos.	808	810
Capacity, gal...........	8	10
W't each, lbs.	21	23
Per dozen	$32.00	35.00
	AIBJ	BAJJ

No. 888—Narrow, 8 gal., made to ride three abreast in ordinary wagon box, otherwise same as No. 808, per dozen ....A I B J $32.00

Nos. 408 and 808 can be supplied with malleable handles when specified without extra charge.

Nos. 305 to 810, inclusive, and Nos. 205 to 210 fitted with patent regular seamless covers—see page 863—will be fitted with sanitary covers when so specified without extra charge.

MILK BOTTLES AND CAPS.

BOTTLES.

ONE-HALF PINT, ONE GROSS; BALANCE ONE-HALF GROSS IN A CRATE AVOID BREAKING CRATES.

BOTTLES.

Plain Heavy Clear Glass, Standard Full Weight and Capacity.

Pints	½	1	2
W't, gro., lbs..	110	165	250
Per dozen	$0.80	.90	1.20
	EJ	EE	JGJ

Strictly F. O. B. Chicago.

CAPS.

Standard Wood Pulp, Waxed.

No. 62—In boxes of 1 M—less quantity not sold—w't per M 1½ lbs., per M ....C J $0.50

No. 62½—In boxes of 5 M, w't per box 13 lbs. ....per M AE $0.38

PACIFIC R R. CANS.

Extra Heavy and Retinned, Solid Plug Covers, Brass Chains.

Nos.	102	103
Capacity, gal.	2	3
W't each, lbs.	7½	8
Per dozen	$18.00	20.00
	AHJJ	AIAJ

FOR FACTORY SHIPMENT ONLY.

FACTORY MILK CANS.

Milwaukee Pattern.   Wisconsin Pattern.

MILWAUKEE PATTERN.

Floating Seamless Cover, Tin Body, Solid Hoops.

Nos.	115	120	130
Capacity, gal..	15	20	30
W't each, lbs..	25	30	35
Each	$4.50★	5.00★	5.75★
	DCBJ	DEFJ	EDJJ

WISCONSIN PATTERN.

Stationary Ventilating Cover, Tin Body, Solid Hoops.

Nos.	215	220	230
Capacity, gal..	15	20	30
W't each, lbs..	25	30	35
Each	$4.50★	5.00★	5.75★
	DCBJ	DEFJ	EDJJ

ROYAL.

Highest Quality Cheese Factory Milk Cans, Stationary Top Cover, Body Swaged to Stop Slopping.

Nos.	315	320	330
Capacity, gal..	20	30	40
W't each, lbs..	29	33	40
Each	$9.50★	11.50★	13.50★
	EGJ	JFIJ	JHAJ

K. D. stock $2.00 less per set.
F. O. B. Detroit, Mich.

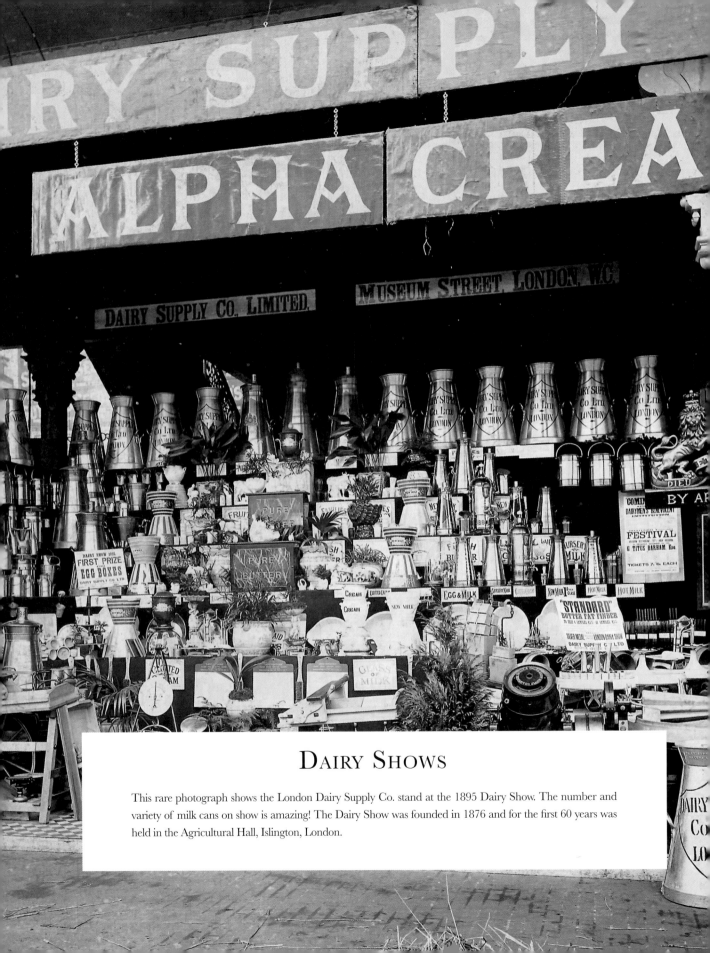

DAIRY SHOWS

This rare photograph shows the London Dairy Supply Co. stand at the 1895 Dairy Show. The number and variety of milk cans on show is amazing! The Dairy Show was founded in 1876 and for the first 60 years was held in the Agricultural Hall, Islington, London.

PROMOTIONAL GIFTS

This terrace house at 13 Rugby Street, London was built circa 1721. The Davies Family had the dairy shop from about 1887. The frontage of French's Dairy survives intact to this day. When it was a dairy they gave away nickel plated brass vesta cases (match cases). This is a very rare survivor from a time when some vesta cases were miniature billboards.

French's Dairy is now a jewellers selling fabulous jewellery.

Photograph kindly provided by Caroline Derry.

THE STORY OF MILK IN COLLECTABLE CARDS

Clover Dairies Limited (London) issued a series of 25 cards (circa 1965) illustrating the story of milk. These four cards show the following: the milk churn loading bay at the farm ; cooling the milk at the farm dairy to as low a temperature as possible; sampling milk at the milk factory to test its hygienic and chemical quality; milk cans from farms arriving at the milk factory.

PATENTS FOR MILK CANS AND A REGISTERED DESIGN

PATENTS

Next page from top left to bottom. A 1910 patent by Leonard R. Steel of Milwaukee (U.S.A.) for a glass lined milk can. The primary object of the invention was to provide a milk can that could be kept in highly sanitary conditions at all times. A further feature is that the lining of glass could be readily and quickly replaced. A simple modifications to a milk can. Filed in 1908 by Alfred Henry Riley (Auckland, New Zealand) the invention relates to billy cans, milk cans and similar items to prevent liquids from slopping down the side of the can. A 1909 patent by George H. Marting (Columbus, Ohio) is for a milk can which is designed to receive milk directly from the cow. An innovative design but probably not well received, especially by the cows. Above a patent for a self-measuring can was filed in 1898 by C.H. Van Alstyne of Manchester, Iowa.

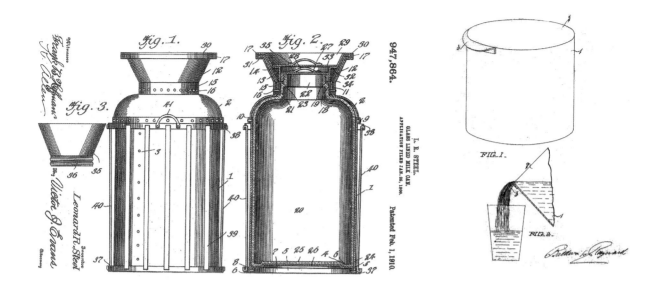

947,864.

L. B. STEEL.
GLASS LINED MILK CAN.
APPLICATION FILED JAN. 26, 1909.

Patented Feb. 1, 1910.

Fig.1.

Fig.2.

Fig.3.

Leonard B. Steel

G. H. MARTING.
MILK CAN.
APPLICATION FILED FEB. 1, 1909.

929,150.

Patented July 27, 1909.

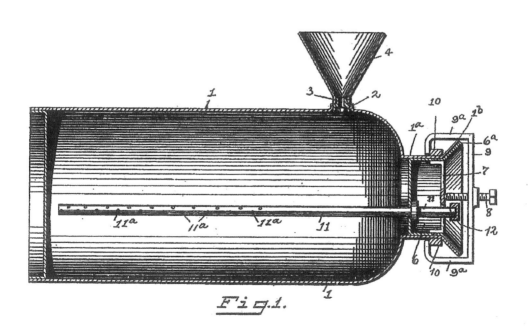

Fig.1.

521974

Side Elevation of Vessel Complete.   *Side Elevation of lid.*   *Plan View of vessel.*

John Newton

Longport. Stoke-on-Trent. Staffordshire. Agent for the Applicants.

A REGISTERED DESIGN

In Britain, the Design Act of 1842 established 13 classes of ornamental designs for articles made of wood, glass, earthenware, paper-hangings, carpets and fabrics. In The National Archives (TNA) at Kew, London, there are registers for each class. These are perhaps the most interesting archives that any researcher could ever wish to consult. Registration No. 521974 in 1909 was for a miniature milk can. This design was later used for souvenirs such as the example shown here.

The example on the right is Goss Ware, just 2 ¾ inches tall (7 cm.) and is from Tunbridge Wells in England. The base mark reads 'Model of a Boulogne Milk Can Rd. No. 521974. Boulogne-sur-mer (France) is famous for its fromages (cheeses).

DO WELL DOUBT NOT
ROYAL TUNBRIDGE WELLS

ACCESSORIES

INSULATION AND AN AERATOR

There are several items that could be called milk can accessories. Above is a rare example of a milk can insulation jacket. It is marked 'Magic Insulation Jacket' and has the Letters N.E.M.P.A., Andover Mass. (USA). Even rarer examples were made of wood.

On the right is an image from a Harvey & Sons Ltd milk can catalogue showing an 'aerator' and a 'strainer'. The aerator is recommended for use where there are many flies.

THE "RV" AERATOR
FOR MILK AND CREAM CANS

The ultimate choice of men who insist on clean superfine cream or milk. Keeps out flies, birds, dogs, vermin, dust, etc. Aerates the cream, allowing a cross current of air to circulate through the can. This Aerator is the cheapest, simplest and most efficient. No need to use insanitary cloths, etc., always handy. Can be in use in less than a minute. Allows the can to be left in the open, no need to place in a sheltered place.

Strainer to use on top of aerator when separating into cream can if flies are around.

———————

Lid fits inside top end. Bottom end fits into the can.

This Aerator is simply a seamless perforated cylinder, tinned after the perforations have been put in. One end fits into the can. Where flies are extremely bad, place the aerator on top of the can, then strainer on top of aerator. No flies can then get into the cream can while separating. Only one strainer necessary, as this can be shifted from can to can.

MADE IN DIFFERENT SIZES TO FIT ALL CANS.

10-in. dia. will fit 12, 10 and 8 gall. Bottle Neck Cans. Price: 4/-
9-in. ,, ,, ,, 6 and 5 ,, ,, ,, ,, Price: 3/9
8-in. ,, ,, ,, 4 and 3 ,, ,, ,, ,, Price: 3/9

Strainer to fit 10-in. diameter Aerator.
     ,, ,, ,, 9-in. ,, ,, } Price: 4/6.
     ,, ,, ,, 8-in. ,, ,,

OTHER SIZES ON APPLICATION.

FUN WITH FUNNELS

In this charming scene, the child on the left is using a funnel (an accessory) while pouring the milk into the milk can. The child on the right is handling two vacuum milking buckets.

This image comes the 1928 cover of the magazine 'The Dairy Farmer'.

5 cents a copy

115

A COLLECTION OF ACCESSORIES

This collection of milk can accessories includes (right bottom) a pair of very rare lifting hooks used to lift the full cans from delivery carts to the upper storey of the dairy factory. The milk scales were made in New York and have a Chatillon's improved circular spring balance to weigh 60 lbs. The milk can dipstick is dated 1937 and was made by the Dairymen's Supply Co., Philadelphia. Three dials measures up to 20, up to 30 or up to 40 quarts. The item on the top left is for pressing lead seals and the wooden hammer was used to help remove and replace lids on milk cans.

PROCESSING AND MAINTENANCE

Up and away

Above is an 1893 illustration of a 'Railway Milk Can Elevator' for lifting cans and delivering contents into tanks for supplying separators. The advertisement says "made any height to order".

On the right is an almost unbelievable lift (elevator) and spiral roller conveyor for storing 500 empty milk cans then loading the cans on to lorries. This was used in England by Cadbury Brothers Ltd., cocoa and chocolate manufacturers. This image was published in the 1931 September issue of *Fawcett's Mechanics and Inventions*.

Milk Cans Loaded by Gravity Power

CLEANING MILK CANS

An early innovative invention took much of the hard work out of cleaning milk cans. This was Pococks's Patent milk can washer. A report in the *Journal of the Royal Agricultural Society of England* for 1882 reads as follows: "The Reading Iron Works Company obtained the Society's Silver Medal for a washing machine for railway milk cans. Two men with the aid of this machine can wash up to 200 cans per hour". That is one every 8 seconds – unbelievable! The price was 38 pounds sterling.

POCOCK'S PATENT MILK CAN WASHER

BRUSH FOR COVER

MILK CANS GALORE

Amidst the clatter of steel against steel, these ten gallon milk cans have arrived at a dairy processing plant cheese factory or creamery. This scene is typical of the period between the 1920s and early 1960s. Each can has the farm number T2. The man on the left was known as a 'sniffer'. The man on the right is taking a milk sample to be sent for a Babcock Butterfat test to determine the value of the milk. This photograph was kindly provided by The National Dairy Shrine, U.S.A.

THE DAIRY FARM AND SOCIAL ASPECTS

THE LOCAL DAIRY FACTORY

In the late nineteenth century and early twentieth century many country dairy factories provided a meeting place for local dairy farmers. This photograph is a rich insight into such occasions where news was exchanged as well as the exchange of farm produce. The photograph (taken in circa 1910) shows large straight-sided milk cans in horse drawn carts at the Staveley Co-op Dairy Company in Canterbury, New Zealand. Farmers were paid on weight of milk supplied.

The photograph was kindly provided by the Old Dairy Factory Gallery at Staveley.

A SPECIAL DAY ON THE FARM - 1935

Some retired dairy farmers have said that the arrival of the first milk can was an occasion to celebrate. This charming photograph was taken in 1935 and shows a very proud family (three generations?) showing smiles of satisfaction. The milk can appears to be shiny and clean. Was this their first milk can (or first can of milk?).

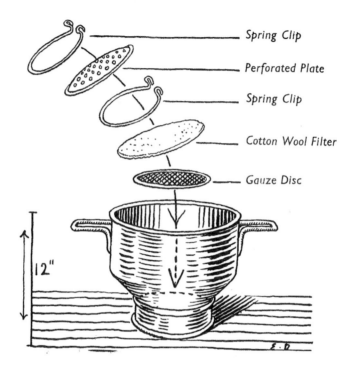

Spring Clip

Perforated Plate

Spring Clip

Cotton Wool Filter

Gauze Disc

12"

FARMCRAFT FOR AMATEURS - 1942

These clearly drawn images are from *A Book of Farmcraft* published by Longmans, Green and Co. Ltd. in 1942. Dedicated 'to our mothers', the book was written for the novice at a time when soldiers, nurses, schoolboys, schoolgirls and all kind of people were doing farm-work for the first time in their lives. The top images shows how to reel a milk can. The milk can is rotated anti-clockwise and notice how the position of the woman's hands change as she takes a few steps forwards.

Above is a strainer and the bottom right is the "interior of a dairy".

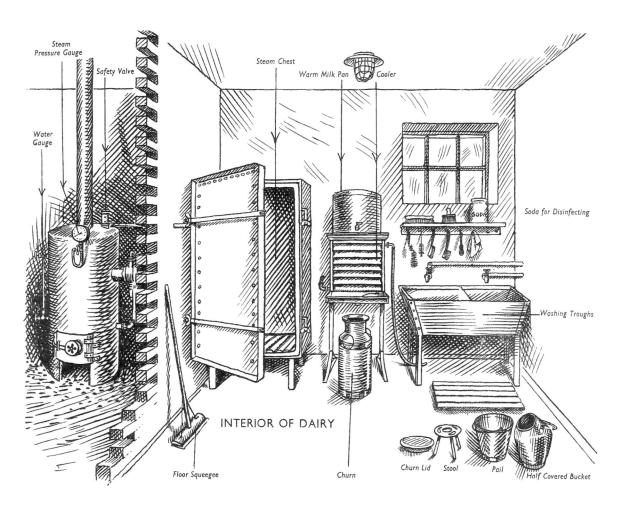

INTERIOR OF DAIRY

Steam
Pressure Gauge

Safety Valve

Water
Gauge

Steam Chest

Warm Milk Pan   Cooler

Soda for Disinfecting

Washing Troughs

Floor Squeegee

Churn

Churn Lid   Stool   Pail   Half Covered Bucket

THE COUNTRY MILK RUN - 1948

In 1948, *TIME* Magazine published this colourful and well-designed advertisement for the National City Bank. The quiet rural scene is dominated by the nine milk cans on the stand with two cans precariously placed on top. Cows graze peacefully in the field next to some farm buildings. In the distance a milk lorry is approaching the milk stand. The picture is a gentle reminder of an unhurried time when milk cans were collected from milk stands at the side of the road. The original painting is by Clarence H. Carter (1904-2000). Carter's paintings during the 1930s and 1940s were typically of rural America.

135

WHAT HAPPENS WHEN THERE'S A MILK STRIKE?

Milk dumping and milk strikes often resulted in emptying milk cans and then scattering them across the countryside. There appear to be four distinct piles of milk cans with a total of over 140 cans. The last of the cans is being emptied with some apparent satisfaction. This photograph, taken in Racine, Wisconsin in about 1934 was kindly provided by the Wisconsin Historical Society. The accompanying text reads "a group of men protesting inadequate payment for dairy products stopped a train, broke open the box cars and dumped milk cans on the tracks".

TRANSPORT

THE MILKMAIDS

The image above was drawn in the second half of the nineteenth century. The artist was either Valentijn BING (1812-1895) or Jan Braet von UBERFELDT (1807-1894). Courtesy of the Nederlands Openluchtmuseum, Arnhem, Netherlands. The description is given as "Girl from the land of Heusden with a copper milk jug on a leather knot on her back". Heusden is a city in the south of the Netherlands that dates back to the 13th century.

On the right is 'Milk below maids' (from the Cries of London). It is one of several pictures by the engraver Luigi Schiavonetti (1765-1810) and painted circa 1793 by F. Wheatley R.A. (1747-1801). The milk cans appear to have no lids. The volume of each milk can is difficult to estimate but appears to be no more than five gallons. If they were five gallons cans, each full can would have weighed 51.6 lbs (23.4 kg.).

Image courtesy of Intaglio-fine-art.com.

Burdens on their heads

Women have carried burdens on the top of their head in many countries for centuries. The image above comes from the 14th Century Luttrell Psalter. It shows sheep being medicated and two women carry pots on their heads, presumably carrying milk back to the farm. Courtesy of the British Library Board.

The photograph on the right is circa 1900. The milk carrier has obviously had much practice in balancing a milk can on a 'cushion' placed on her head. Her skill is quite remarkable as she pours milk from through a tap on the can into a small jug. The slightly dented milk can was probably made of tin and probably held at least two gallons (20.6 lbs, 9.3 kg).

The image is from an undated stereoscope slide by the Keystone View Co., copyrighted Underwood & Underwood.

The milkmen

Above is William Fryer. He was born in 1843 and at the age of eight commenced work on his father's farm in England. This backyard garden photograph was taken after 1874, when he worked for R. Higgs and Sons. He has a yoke around his neck with two leather straps holding two large carriers' pails. Each pail in turn has several hand cans attached. He looks quite relaxed, suggesting that the cans are empty. The volume of the carriers' pails may have been as much as five gallons. When full, the two cans combined would have weighed as much as 103 lbs. (47 kgs.).

Mr. Bob Malcolm kindly provided the photograph which appears in 'The British Milkman' by Tom Phelps, published by Shire Publications in 2010 and used with permission of Bloomsbury Publishing, Inc.

On the right is a milkman from Bhutan with bamboo milk cans. The image is from an undated postcard but thought to date from about 1910.

7351.　A Boothea Milkman.

145

THE MILK CARRIAGE

On the right four men and two boys are posing for the photographer in this carefully orchestrated scene. The poster (top left) has the words 'One Tree Hill Dairy' above a hill with a single tree. Perhaps this postcard photograph was to appear in some form of advertising. Photographs of this ingenious means of transporting milk cans are rarely seen. The One Tree Hill Dairy was in Auckland, New Zealand. One tree Hill is a well-known landmark. The cans on the trolleys (or carriages) have straight sides and a lid with an aerator on the top. Note the kettles or carriers' pails carried by the boy on the left. This image is from an undated '*Marathon*' postcard from about 1900.

The illustration above is from W. Lock's *Book of Farm Management*. The description reads; 'a milk carriage from about 1800'. The date seems rather early for a milk can of this shape and design.

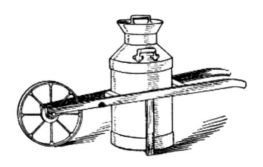

WHEELBARROWS AND A MILK CAN BARROW

Between 1909 and 1937, *Popular Mechanics* included several articles describing how to modify wheelbarrows. These were aimed at dairy farmers to make it easier for them to transport full dairy cans from the farm dairy to the milk stand at the side of the road.

The milk can barrow on the right is made entirely of steel including the wheels. Presumably this was not suitable for use over rough ground and would therefore have been used in the dairy factories.

PERAMBULATORS

The next step up from pushing a milk carriage was to push a milk perambulator. These were to become perhaps the most common method of delivering milk in London in the late 19th Century. The Dairy Supply Co., London offered many models in their catalogues, including the 'milk trolley' (milk carriage).

PERAMBULATORS.

All made in well-seasoned timber, each painted in the best style and any colour, and written in gold letters.

Nos. 1 and 2.

No. 1.—Wheels 24 inches in diameter, with Iron Rails, ordinary Axles, and made to carry 50-quart Churn .. £4 15s

No. 2.—Same as above, but with Brass Rails, Patent Axles, 27 inch Wheels. To carry 50, 66, or 80 quart Churn .. £8

No. 3.—Brass Rails and Margin round Oval, Name Board, Patent Axles, 30 inch Wheels. To carry 50, 66, or 80 quart Churn £9 10s.

With Iron Rails £9

No. 3.

No. 4.—Two-wheeler, Patent Axles, bold Side Boards, Brass Rails for Cans, 42 inch Wheels. To carry 66 quart Churn. These run easier than those with three wheels, and are much in vogue with Town Dairies .. ., ... £9

No. 5.—Without Legs, same as used by Callow Park .. £7 10s.

Swing Box for carrying Butter, Eggs, and Books, extra 10/-.

No. 4.

The above Prices include Painting and Picking out, any colour, and with sixty $1\frac{1}{2}$-inch Gold Letters. All are well Varnished, and finished in a workmanlike manner.

For Churns for these Perambulators see opposite page.

MILK TROLLEY AND CAN.

10 Gallon	..	..	..	..	..	£3	0 0
12 ,,	..	..	..	..	..	3	5 0
14 ,,	..	..	..	..	..	3	17 6
20 ,,	..	..	..	..	..	4	12 6
With Tap, extra	..	..	..	..		5	6
Hand Can	..	..	..	..	..	6	0

Made in all sizes.

These Milk Trolleys are very suitable for conveying quantities of Milk between Cowshed and Dairy, also in proving new rounds payable before going to expense of Perambulator.

MILK PERAMBULATORS READY FOR DELIVERY

This photograph on the bottom right shows a team of milkmen (all men?) with their milk perambulators in London. They were distributing milk for Long & Pocock. Note the single delivery can in each perambulator and the rows of hand cans attached. Long & Pocock had their dairy shop in Uxbridge Road, West Ealing. They later amalgamated with United Dairies. Was the policeman on the far right there to guide the milkmen between the traffic?

The photograph belonged to the late Brian Pocock (Grandson of Walter Pocock (1879-1939).

The 1908 photograph on the top right shows a group of boys about to deliver milk before going to school. The size of the milk perambulators and the delivery cans are suitably smaller for the boys.

The images are reproduced here with permission of Tom Phelps (author of *The British Milkman* published by Shire Publications) and with permission of Bloomsbury Publishing Plc.

THE MILK MUST GET THROUGH

Published in 1917 in *The Illustrated War News*, this shows a steel-helmeted milk seller on her morning rounds in Rheims, Northern France. Despite the bombings, butchers, bakers and milk-sellers continued their rounds. Note the shape and size of the seven or eight milk cans. Presumably each can has a tap as shown. Notice also the white cloths (in place of lids) which presumably were a means of keeping the milk open to the air while protecting contamination.

155

MILK TRICYCLE

This extremely rare photograph (from a glass slide) shows a milk tricycle and well-dressed rider. The photograph was taken in the late 19th Century. In 1877, George Liddiard, cowkeeper, Kensington, London had been charged with having an infected place. The tricycle has the typical delivery can together with an array of hand cans. This must surely have made delivery rounds much easier than pushing perambulators or hand carts.

157

Dog carts

Dogs have long been used to pull carts and sledges in both peace and war. In Belgium, dog milk carts have long been a common sight. Note the shape of the brass milk cans with their long narrow necks and round lids.

This image comes from the 1935 *Hutchinson's Popular and Illustrated Dog Encyclopedia* and is attributed to Mondiale.

HORSE DRAWN MILK CARTS

Milk carts such as this were beautifully decorated. Presumably the owners were very proud of them and their horses. C.W. Baker was a tobacconist, confectioner, dairyman and grocer in London. Milk was delivered twice daily. The typical delivery can shines brightly in the cart. Presumably a kettle and small hand cans would be on the floor of the cart.

Image from an undated photograph on card.

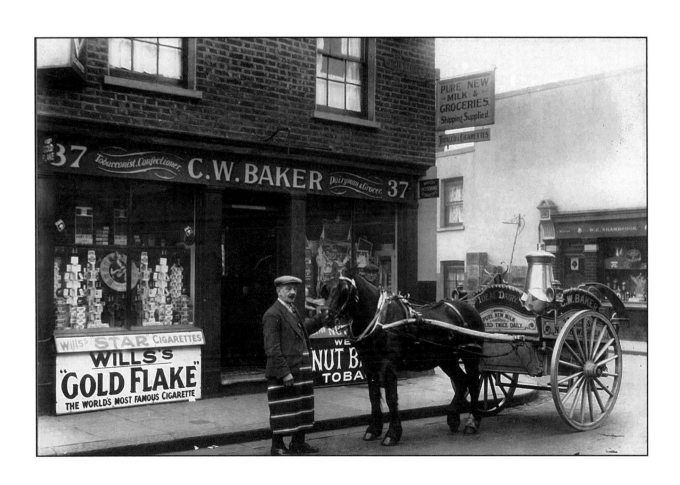

161

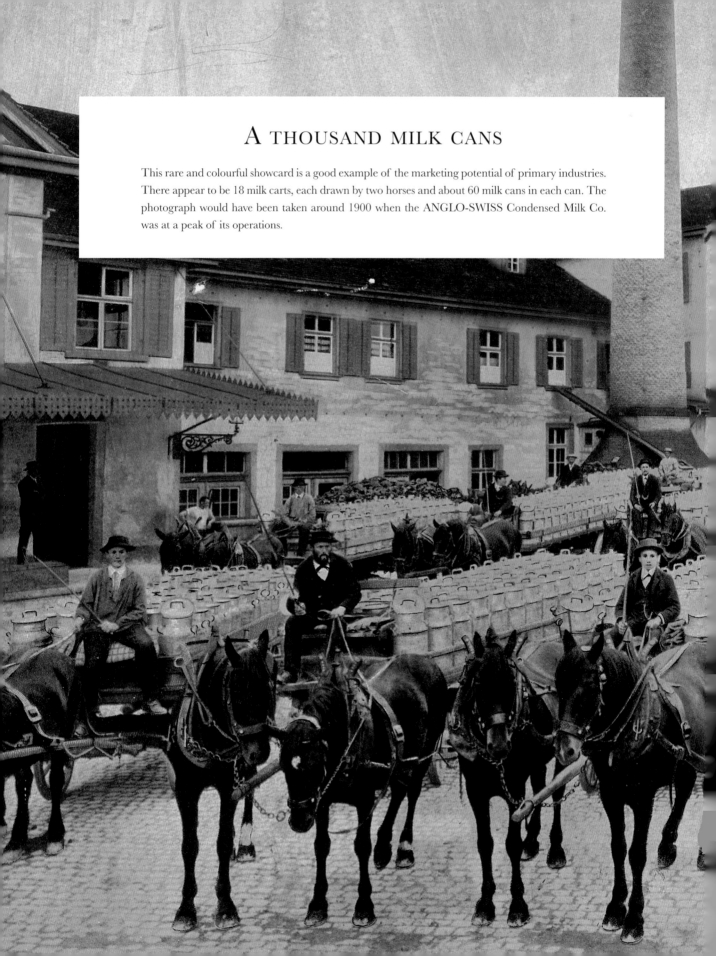

A THOUSAND MILK CANS

This rare and colourful showcard is a good example of the marketing potential of primary industries. There appear to be 18 milk carts, each drawn by two horses and about 60 milk cans in each can. The photograph would have been taken around 1900 when the ANGLO-SWISS Condensed Milk Co. was at a peak of its operations.

BOATS BRINGING FRESH MILK FOR CADBURY'S MILK CHOCOLATE.
*There are 1½ glasses of fresh full cream milk in
every ½-lb. of Cadbury's Milk Chocolate.*
4788

DAIRY BOATS

Above: Canal boats bringing fresh milk in large milk churns to Cadbury's factory in England. From an undated and unattributed postcard.

Opposite page: The Mokau River in the North Island of New Zealand has a very long history of river boats. This image shows a post crane with milk cans loading a river boat. From an undated and unattributed photograph.

ON YOUR BIKE

Transporting milk cans on bicycles or motor cycles is common in India. Notice the two similar milk cans above and the contrasting three large brass cans on the right. The above image is part of a photograph by Greg O'Beirne, a file from Wikimedia Commons.

The photograph on the right is used with kind permission of Lucy Patterson.

MILK CAN LORRY WITH THE 'EMPTIES'

This spectacular load of neatly stacked empty milk cans was for the Dargaville Northern Wairoa Co-op Dairy Co., in New Zealand. All the milk cans look similar in design but there are at least two with flat lids. Note the solid wheels on the vehicle.

Dargaville photographer Mr. D.N. Whitburn is accredited this photograph. The image is used here with kind permission of *New Zealand Memories Magazine* and Mr. Brian McClintock.

HENRI NESTLE'S STEAM POWERED MILK LORRY

This magnificent machine must have attracted lots of attention as it hissed and rattled over cobbled roads. Notice the very tidy rows of milk cans, small on the top and large below. Tutbury, Burton-on-Trent, is in England.   The make of the vehicle and the photographer are unknown (taken circa 1901?).

The image is from an undated photograph.

171

DESTINED TO MAKE CHOCOLATE

This photograph shows a Hershey Chocolate Co. truck collecting milk. All of the milk cans seem similar and have unusually long necks. The Hershey Community Archives suggest a date of about 1918, but are unable to provide any information about the make or model of the vehicle. Hershey's is one of the largest chocolate manufacturers in North America and was founded in 1894 by Milton S. Hershey (1857-1945).

The National Dairy Shrine (USAS) kindly provided the photograph.

'DRINKA PINTA MILKA DAY'

Many readers today will recall the Ford Thames Trader Milk Lorry between 1957-1965. The catch phrase 'drinka pinta milka day' may also be remembered. Notice the milk cans have 'mushroom' lids.

The image is from an undated photograph on card. The photographer is unknown.

175

FRENCH RAILWAYS BETTER THAN ENGLISH RAILWAYS FOR TRANSPORTING MILK CANS

Very early on, railways were recognized for their role in distributing agriculture products. In 1867 there was much discussion in London about how best to transport milk cans by rail. It was reported that in France the milk cans were smaller (20 litres) and were made with a double case. This meant that the cans could be easily stacked in the two storeyed railway wagons and that the cans were insulated. Why was this design not adopted in England?

The images are from the London *Proceedings of the Journal of Society and Arts* (1867).

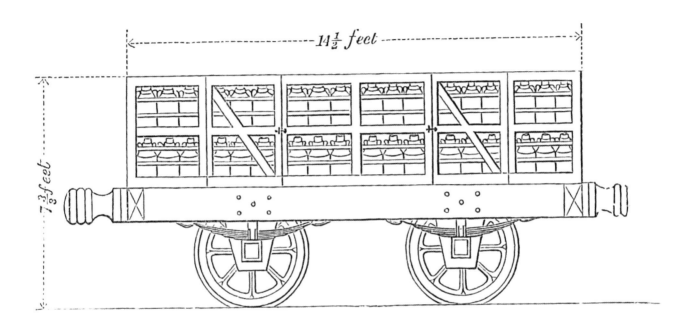

A Railway milk dock in Australia circa 1910

These were the early days of milk was collection from many small railway stations. This is the milk dock redistribution area at the Tongala railway station in the Goulburn Valley, Victoria, Australia.

This image is from the collection held by the Museum of Victoria.

Notice the design of the milk cans. They are cylindrical with no neck and collapsible handles. The example on the right holds five gallons (the cans on the milk dock are larger). The letters 'WAY' are stamped within a circle on both the lid and the side of the can. The brass badge reads 'D. Weeding Koriella'.

Railway milk docks in London

The sight of hundreds of milk churns (circa 1914) at the London railway stations must have been very impressive, while the sounds of clanking metal cans would have been deafening. These were commonly known as 'milk churns' because the design was based in part on the old conical shaped butter churns.

The image on the right is with permission of the STEAM Picture Library.

The image above is from Helena Wojtczal's 2005 book '*Railway Women – Exploitation, Betrayal and Triumph in the Workplace*, published by Hastings Press. It is a lovely reminder that women have always worked on the railways.

The Silent Milk Churn—An improved milk churn has just been invented with rubber tyres round the base and lid to prevent the rattling that is so disturbing in the early morning to sleepers living near a dairy or station. See page

SILENCE OF THE MILK CHURNS

In England and France during the early 1930s, the newspapers published many letters complaining about the 'rattling', 'dumping', 'bumping' and 'clanging' of milk churns while they were being transported and delivered. The courts were on the side of complainants and subsequently the 'silent milk churn' was invented in 1923. Thereafter, silent milk churns were widely advertised.

A *SILENT* MILK-CHURN AT LAST

STOP THAT NOISE THAT ANNOYS

clattering churns can be avoided

SEE STAND No.

215 - 6

special features:—

- Longer wear owing to shock absorbing silencer

- This 17 Gall. Churn occupies less space than the old type, thus giving more churns per load

This Silencer reduces vibration on Milk, prevents damage to floors, and reduces overhead charges generally.

SILENT MILK CHURNS Ltd.
NORTHCLIFFE HOUSE, DERBY

Upcycling - A New Lease of Life

NEW USES LIMITED ONLY BY ONE'S IMAGINATION

One of the most common examples of milk can upcycling is letterboxes. Indeed a whole volume could be devoted to milk can letterboxes. Garden seats and even indoor milk can seats are also very common. Less common is the conversion to a soft drink dispenser. Perhaps examples of upcycled milk cans could be the focus of a new study by collectors and material designers.

LIGHT BY MILK CAN

The milk can shape has inspired designers to use it for light shades or to make light shades in the form of milk cans. The example on the right is from India and is a design by the Sarthak Sahil Design Co. Other designs include homemade standard lamps.

189

'WOODEN TOPS'

It's not unusual to find old milk cans that have had their lids replaced with wooden tops. These milk cans were converted for use as bins for wheat, flour, bread, and dog biscuits, the number of uses is limited only by your imagination. The conical shape of the example on the right is very unusual. It holds three gallons and has J.B. MacEwan & Co., Ltd. Dairy Specialist (New Zealand) on the brass (lozenge) disc.

MILK CAN ART

Arts and crafts are alive and well

Restoring, cleaning then painting old milk cans is very popular. Most examples become works of art. The designs range from abstract, with just one or two colours, to detailed farmyard scenes. Most are unsigned. On the next page (top center) the image is by Glenys Le Couteur and the title of the artwork is 'Waiting for the Ladies'.

The can on the top right is painted in the folk art style of Yoka Van Den Brink using Hindeloopen techniques and Sunday colours. Circa 1993.

MILK CANS AND THE ARTS

SOUVENIRS- REMINDERS OF JOYFUL OCCASIONS

In 1899, a play in four acts, *The Dairy Farm* was performed at Haverly's Theatre, New York. The play ran from September 1899 with 82 performances. The play was written by Mrs. Archie Cowper (aka Eleanor Merron). This miniature milk can was given to every patron on the occasion of the 50th performance. This is possibly the only example of a souvenir milk can celebrating the performance of a play. The can is just 3 ½ inches (8.8 cm.) tall.

LA BASSE-NORMANDIE PITTORESQUE
1780 — Voyons Louis, tiens té coume
y faut et n'fai po d'grimaches.

Collection L. G. B., Saint-Pierre-Église

POSTCARDS — MOMENTS IN TIME CAPTURED FOREVER

The cans on the top right are the typical railway churns (cans). The artist, Donald McGill (1875-1913), is well known for his artwork on seaside postcards. The note on the back of the card reads: "Wednesday 28-7-26. Dear Lilian, Thanks for the card I received this morning. I have posted photos this morning, & I hope they will arrive quiet (sic) safe & sound. With love from Kathy. Have you wrote to Beryl H. yet?" The card on the bottom right shows a "daily scene in the capital of Belgium where the milk inspector is testing the quality of the milk'. Right middle is a scene from Ireland with milk cans being taken to the creamery. The above is a scene from Lower Normandy.

CHRISTMAS CARD MILKMAID

It is very rare to find milk cans on Christmas cards. This is an exception. The little girl is decanting milk from a dipper into a one pint hand can. A kettle milk can is at her feet. Artistic licence has been used because it would be almost impossible for a girl of this size to carry two full kettles on her yoke.

This card is in the collection of the Library of Birmingham, England.

Paintings of milk cans

Milk cans were frequently the sole focus of paintings. The winter scene 'Waiting' on the right is a 1990 Giclee on canvas by Canadian artist Eleanor McDonald www.mcdonaldart.com. The mushroom shaped lid of the milk can is resting on the snow.

The painting above is a water colour by New Zealand artist Adrienne Pavelka and the title is 'Uncle Fred's milk can'. This painting was exhibited at the Ashburton Society's Annual Exhibition in 1985 where she was a guest artist. 'Uncle Fred' was her father's cousin, Fred Pavelka, who farmed and ran a horse riding school at View Hill near Oxford, New Zealand.

E.J. McDonald '90

1/75 Eleanor Joy McDonald

MILK CAN SCULPTURES

The sculpture on the right by Eileen MacDonagh is a "well-loved feature on the Mallow Road, Co. Cork, Ireland. The milk cans are made from limestone and are about six feet tall. The sculpture above is a 2010 Monument to the ordinary (Milk Can). Made of steel, 12 feet tall.

With permission of Michael Johnson (University of Puget Sound, Washington, U.S.A.) MichaelJohnsonSculpture.com.

207

Hidden in milk cans

The second part of the Warsaw Ghetto Underground Archives was hidden in these two milk cans. These cans (MZIHB-650/4-5) are from the collections of the Emanuel Ringelblum Jewish Historical Institute, Warsaw.

Image kindly provided by the Emanuel Ringelblum Jewish Historical Institute.

IN THE IMAGE OF THE MILK CAN

A MATERIAL DESIGNER'S DREAM

The typical milk can shape has become a design icon for many well-known household items. These are just six examples. On the right: New Zealand Chocolate Roses 'n' Castles, Canal Art, Dunedin; Blue Stilton Cheese pot London Pottery; Swiss Chocolates; 'Chupa Chups' can.

Above: a copper tea canister; a bird nesting box.

213

Milk can architecture

On the right is the 30 foot high Salvador's Ice Cream building located in South Dartmouth, Massachusetts, U.S.A.

Above is the 28 feet tall 'Little man ICE CREAM' building in the form of a large milk can is a well-known building in Denver, Colorado. The Building is a Registered Trademark of Little Man ICE CREAM LLC.

Both images courtesy of RoadsideArchitecture.com.

MINIATURES AND TOY MILK CANS

ORNAMENTS AND DESK ACCESSORIES

Time and time again, the typical milk can shape has been used for ornaments and writing desk accessories. On the right is a nineteenth century pounce pot (used to dispense fine sand or powder to help dry ink), a miniature silver Guernsey milk pot; a Royal Crown Derby Ornament; an 1891 silver glue (mucilage) pot.

Above is a miniature dairy perambulator. Below is a cruet set.

MATCH HOLDERS — A DAY TO DAY NECESSITY

From circa 1830 to 1920, match holders were an essential part of everyday life. As well as ordinary match box, novelty makers and silversmiths turned their hand to making attractive match holders. The one on the left is in the form of a hand can, in the middle a small delivery can, and on the right a stylised milk can.

SOUVENIRS

This delightful blue and white figure (on the right) depicting a dog cart and milk maid looks like Delft ware. It is earthenware or creamware and was made around 1900 as a souvenir for the tourist market. It was possibly made in Belgium (or even France or Germany). The history of the dog milk carts includes many souvenirs including the small badge Above).

Dairy Cart,

№ 94
DAIRY CART.

A TOY MILK CART AND MILK TRUCK

Toys advertised in the 1907 Army and Navy Stores (London) catalogue included this delightful horse and dairy cart (above) . The description mentions 'iron wheels, a churn and filler'. The painted version was priced at 13 shillings and nine pence. Dairy carts would have been very familiar to children of that time. What small child would not love this toy?

This Tri-ang diesel milk truck with eight milk cans was a firm favourite during the late 1950s. At sixteen inches long, it was a large toy and very colourful with its red cab and blue deck. A popular toy for children and adults.

MILK CAN GAMES, SPORTS AND ENTERTAINMENT

Milk Can

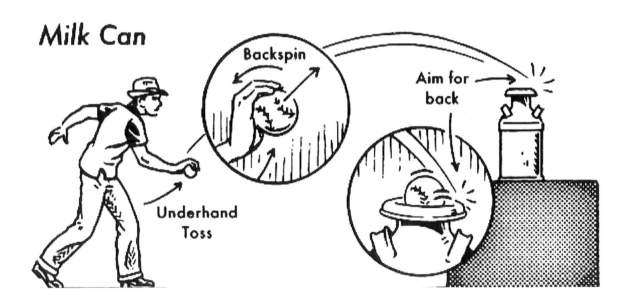

Backspin

Underhand Toss

Aim for back

THE GREAT ESCAPE

The photograph above, taken around 1908, shows the Houdini performing his great milk can escape. From the American Variety Stage: *Vaudeville and Popular Entertainment*. 1870-1920. Library of Congress.

The photograph on the right shows Harry Houdini's milk can being unloaded at the Outagamie Museum by two Museum staff in 1989. Photograph by Ed Deschler. Copyright by The Associated Press.

Milk Can Racing

Churn rolling has long been practiced in Tipperary Town, Ireland where they have the Tipperary Churn Rolling Association. The churns are 30-40 years old and weigh 45 kg. when empty. Manipulation of a full churn is not a simple task. The 20 gallon churn was later replaced by the lighter aluminium ten gallon milk churn.

This photograph was taken in 2015 and kindly supplied by Kieran Maguire, Manager of the Tipperary Co-op.

SPORTS TROPHIES: OF AN IMITATION KIND

A milk can for an imitation of the famous World Rugby Cup? In the small of Kurow in the south Island of New Zealand, they have every reason to be proud of their contribution to Rugby. This photograph was taken in 2015 when Ritchie McCaw led the All Blacks in their successful bid to retain The Webb Ellis Cup (Rugby World Cup). The upturned gold painted milk can, with a few adornments, sits proudly in the foreground of the image of Kurow's rugby hero.

NOSTALGIA:
SENTIMENTAL YEARNING
FOR THE PAST

COUNTRY NOSTALGIA

This painting is aptly called 'The Dairy Cans'. It is by Maurice Harvey and was the sixth issue in a Country Nostalgia series by W.S. George, makers of fine china. The handles of the cans protrude from the shoulders.

237

MILK CAN (CHURN) STANDS

Fast disappearing, these once common features in the countryside are now attracting the attention. Many people would like to see them restored. Right above is the majestic milk churn stand at Old Abbey Farm, Pontrydfendigaid, Wales. Below right is the milk churn stand on Sheep's Head Peninsula, West Cork, Ireland. Above is the stand at Dunbeacon, Mizen Peninsula, Wesr Cork, Ireland. The first image from 'People's Collection Wales (Casgliad y Werin Cymru).

The latter two images kindly provided by Amanda Clarke.

RESTORATION

In these photographs there are examples of milk carts that have been restored, a restored milk carriage, and a railway station decorated with newly painted milk cans on a trolley. Top right is unattributed. Right bottom shows Haverthwaite Station, England (Bob Malcolm photograph). Top left shows a cart with creamery cans in Clonakilty, copyright Kenny Allen. Right above is a photograph by Bob Malcolm showing a restored milk carriage (carrier).

MODERN MILK CANS

MILK CANS FOR THE GOAT HERDS

In this image, goat's milk is being poured from one milk can into another. Whereas milk cans may no longer be used for dairy herds in many countries, there is a demand for cans to cater for the goat herds in New Zealand.

This image was kindly provided by Annabel Langbein Media. Annabel Langbein (The Free Range Cook) is a New Zealand celebrity cook, food writer and publisher.

NEW MILK CANS FOR SALE

Plastic and stainless steel. What else is there to be said?

THERE IS A LOT TO BE SAID! THERE ARE NEW AND INNOVATIVE DESIGNS FOR MODERN MILK CANS

For example, the Mazzi (derived from the Kiswahili word for milk, maziwa) was created by Global Good (a collaboration between Bill Gates and Intellectual Ventures). It's a plastic 10-litre container designed for carrying milk in under-developed places. It has an ultra-wide mouth (a huge design challenge), so that farmers can clean the inside of the container with ease. There are notches on the side so that the Mazzi may be tied to a bike or slung over the shoulder. The Mazzi container is made of durable, food-grade plastic that can be dropped or kicked without breaking. The lid is tethered to the body of the container. A black funnel with a sieve-like opening fits on the top of the Mazzi. Images courtesy of Global Good Intellectual Ventures. www.intellectualventureslab.com/invent/building-the-mts   accessed January 2018.

Now that is something to celebrate!

248

Appendices

Milk cans: collecting, care, and display

I have collected, cherished, and studied milk cans for many years. This area of study has often been met with slight ridicule. As one public figure once said to me "Well, I suppose it's at least as sensible as studying ancient Greek pottery."

At other times, when I've traveled around the world with a large milk can as excess luggage, I have caused some amusement. However, I have found airlines and railways to be most helpful with the transport of milk cans.

My collecting and studying of milk cans has even attracted the attention of a news reporter in India who worked for the *Daily News & Analysis* (dna). The result was a full page spread devoted to various activities including the collecting and studying of milk cans. Is it so unusual to collect milk cans?

A question I am often asked therefore is "why collect and study milk cans?" The answer is that as far as I am aware it has not been done extensively before. Few books have information about 'dairy bygones' including some types of milk cans. The use and design of milk cans is part of our social history.

The condition of old milk cans ranges from rusting remains to those which appear to be in a relatively new condition (despite the fact that they may have been in use for decades). Steel cans with little or no rust may be given a light polish with steel wool then coated in good quality furniture wax or wax that is recommended for stone surfaces. Cans with a mild amount of rust can be cleaned with fine wire wool then coated with wax.

Cans with moderate amounts of rust can be cleaned with emery paper or, if necessary a hand held wire brush, or even occasionally a wire brush in an angle grinder. When doing this work, eyes, ears and hands need to be protected.

Cans with severe rust or even with those with a few holes can be given a new lease of life. Often the bottoms of cans have rusted away but these can be replaced by a metal worker or welder. Very rusty cans can be treated by careful sand-blasting. This is a specialist task and needs to be done by a reputable sand-blasting or powder blasting service. All badges (brass labels) should be removed before this treatment. This can be done by softening the solder underneath the badge with an electrical paint stripper. The badges can be replaced with strong adhesive. As soon as possible after treatment the can should be waxed, oiled or painted.

Copper and brass badges need special care. Some people prefer to not clean them. Others use brass and copper cleaning materials. The painted numbers need extra special care so as not to damage them and can be protected with a coating of wax.

The popularity of garden art spans centuries and currently is very popular. Two or three milk cans as decorative items in the garden or near the house can complement planted beds, lawns and trees. Milk cans that once belonged to the family farm have particularly nostalgic value. This is especially so for families where brass milk cans and pots are never sold and are passed from one generation to another.

The restoration of milk cans is, for many reasons, extremely popular. Perhaps the best example of restoration was the true story of 500 old milk cans being 'resurrected'. In his book '*Something Strange Happened on my Way to the Zoo*', Mike Thomas wrote along the following lines "A local farmer told me that soon milk churns would be a thing of the past. What bothered me was that milk churns, symbols of rural life, might never be seen by new generations. That would be like tearing the pages out of history books. A week later I signed a contract with the Milk Marketing Board and bought five hundred redundant churns". Following that purchase Mike Thomas decided to enhance the charm of the churns with copper and brass plating. His anecdote ends "I like brass and copper and I know a man who could do it".

In some recent correspondence with Mike Thomas he wrote the following: "Of the 500, some were too dilapidated to be able to resurrect. However, our process involved some being cut down in size then the job of cleaning, copper and brass plating was devised and completed before the polishing process (by hand and much sweat) .. resulting in a beautiful piece of sculpture with a fascinating and interesting (in many cases) history (see below).

All the churns were stamped with the maker's names and addresses. These were crafted onto the churns and lids. The task was to find the correct lids to correspond to the churns and reunite them since over many years of use and cleaning they had become separated.

Many years after I ceased to refurbish and sell the churns, I found one in an antique shop 200 miles from my home in Cornwall. The lid was stamped with PRIMOSE DAIRY HAYLE but the churn stamp read TOTNESS DAIRY. By coincidence I had given a present to my mother of a milk churn and when she passed away I brought it home as a memory of her. The lid was stamped with TOTNESS DAIRY and the churn read PRIMROSE DAIRY HAYLE. I bought the one from the antique shop, reunited both lids and churns and sold the TOTNES churn to my wife's hairdresser who cherishes it for its beauty, history and the delightful story of the reunited churn.

'Marriages', 'reproductions', and 'mystery' cans

An example of a reproduction milk can is a conical shaped brass can with the engraved words 'Guaranteed Pure Milk' and 'Skidmore & Son (England)'. These were copied in about 2006 and made in three sizes. They might have been made in India or China. Counter dairy pans have also been reproduced many times.

Old milk cans are not uncommon, although unusual shapes and sizes are difficult to find. There are some old containers that look like milk cans but are more likely to be petroleum tins or certified measuring containers. Night cans can also be confused with old milk cans. Night cans were used for removing night soil (human faeces) from properties that were not connected to sewage systems.

Occasionally 'mystery' cans are found. An example shown here (opposite page) is a heavy copper one quart can. The construction and crude lettering suggests an old milk container. The word 'milk' appears on a brass rim together with what appears to be a random set of letters. The mystery will probably never be solved.

Dairy collectables

For the collector of 'kitchenalia' there is a cornucopia of items awaiting discovery, research and loving care. Likewise, the history of dairying, dairy-related items and advertising spin-offs offer a veritable and fruitful area for study and collecting. For example, old milk bottles, old milk churns, and wooden milk buckets are all very collectable.

In the U.S.A., the first prototype for a milk bottle was a wooden bottle made in 1884. According to the Potsdam Public Museum (New York) the idea of a milk bottle was prompted by a little girl accidently dropping her rag doll into a ten gallon milk can. Dr. Thatcher, a Potsdam pharmacist, rescued the doll. That event prompted him to design a milk bottle and he made his first example on a lathe. With a year or two glass bottles for milk delivery had been invented. For decades, glass bottles were used time and time again but then

the 'throw-away society' eventually took over with the use of disposable containers.

There are hundreds if not thousands of collectors of milk bottles around the world. Some collections are as large as 2,000 bottles, even up to 15,000 bottles. There are milk bottle collectors clubs and in the USA there is a National Association of Milk Bottle Collectors. Milk bottle collecting takes advantage of social media; there are collectors' guides to milk bottles, manuals and price guides. Why are milk cans not collected with the same enthusiasm as milk bottles?

Many cream pots for potted or preserved cream survive from the Victorian and Edwardian eras. With a brand name and the dairy name on these small stone-ware pots, they are very collectable compared to milk bottles much less seems to be written about them.

Butter churns are also very collectable. Churning milk to make butter goes back centuries and a major development was the invention of the wooden milk churn. Towards the end of the nineteenth century, there were applications for hundreds of improvements to milk churns. Some were very unusual such as those combining rocking chairs with churns. The term 'churn' was also adopted in England for an early form of metal milk container because the shape resembled the old manual wooden milk churn.

One other very collectable milk-related item is the mechanical separator. The names De Laval and Alfa-Laval have been associated with separators since the 1870s. Not only are the old separators collector's items but De Laval also produced promotional items such as wall mounted miniature cream separators.

For centuries, wooden milk pails have been in common use. However there were always problems with hygiene. In 1876, articles appeared in both *The Farmer's Magazine* (Britain) and *The New England Farmer* (U.S.A.) about the lack of cleanliness of wooden milk pails and how it was impossible to keep them 'sweet'. It was proposed that tin pails that fitted neatly into the wooden pails be adopted.

Some of the oldest accessories are the dairy yokes (shoulder yokes). These were made of light wood, concave at the centre to fit across the shoulders. Adjustable chains were fitted at each end to attach the milk cans.

From the author's family photograph album 'one'

RESOURCES

Specialist dealers

The Antique Dispensary Ltd., England. Mr. Laurence Cooper is the purveyor.

Pearmont Dairy Antiques, De Pere, Wisconsin 54115.

Raflees barn find bygones store on eBay. Based in Devon, U.K.

Museums and shows

There are dairy museums in many parts of the world. The following are just a few examples.

France

The world's largest museum of milk and cheese is the Andre Besnier Museum of milk in Laval, France (Musee du Lactopole Andre Besnier a Laval.

India

The Dairy Museum within the Campus of Amul Dairy at Anand.

Ireland.

Old Irish Ways. Near Bruff, Limerick.

U.S.A.

Doug & Linda's Dairy Antique Site.

National Dairy Shrine Museum and Hoard Historical Museum, Fort Atkinson, U.S.A.

Pasto Agriculture Museum, Pennsylvania State University.

The All-American Dairy Show.

U.K.

Acton Scott Museum and Historic Working Farm, Shropshire, England.

Museum of English Rural Life, University of Reading, England.

Further reading

Atkins, P.J. 1980. The retail milk trade in London, c. 1790-1914. *The Economic History Review*, New Series, Vol. 33 (4), p. 522-537.

Belloin, J.C. 1988. Milk and dairy products: production and processing costs. FAO, Rome.

Benoit, G. 2013. *Ardeche-Drome*: Bidons sans frontières. Glenat.

Baird, J.S. 1994. *Hoard's Dairyman. Dairy Collectables*. W.D. Hoard & Sons Co., Fort Atkinson, U.S.A.

Brown, J. 2012. *Farming in the 1920s and '30s*. Shire Publications, Oxford, U.K.

Crossley, E.L. (ed.). 1959. *The United Kingdom Dairy Industry*. U.K. Dairy Association, London.

Dillon, John J. 1941. Seven Decades of Milk. A history of New York's dairy industry. Reprinted 2013 by Read Books Ltd.

Davies, P. 2009. *Lost London 1870-1945*. English Heritage.

Fussell, G.E. *The English Dairy Farmer 1500-1900*. 1966. Frank Cass & Co., Ltd., London.

Greenhill, M. and Dunbar, E. 1942. *A Book of Farmcraft*. Longmans, Green & Co., London.

Ingram, A. 2008. *Dairying Bygones*. Shire Publications Ltd., Oxford, U.K.

Jones, C.M. (ed.) 2006. *One Hundred Years of Inquiry and Innovation. An illustrated history of the American Dairy Science Association*. Banta Publications, U.S.A.

Mayhew, H. 1851. *London Labour & the London Poor*, Volume 1. Dover Publications (1968).

Munns, R.T. 1986. *Milk Churns to Merry-Go-Round. A Century of Train Operation*. David & Charles, London.

Nimmo, R. 2010. *Milk, Modernity and the Making of the Human - Purifying the Social.* Routledge, London.

Phelps, T. 2010. *The British Milkman.* Shire Publications, Oxford, U.K.

Phelps, T. 2015. *Britain's Wartime Milkmen.* Chaplin Books, Gosport, U.K.

Piper, C. 1995. Billy Can to Carton. *The History of 'Gisborne Milk'.* Gisborne Milk Co-op Ltd., New Zealand.

Pirtle, T.R. 1926. *History of the Dairy Industry.* Mojonnier Bros. Company, Chicago, Illinois.

Roberts, S. 1977. Bygones from the dairy. *Art & Antiques*, June 11, pp. 32-34.

Ward & Lock. 1881. *Ward & Lock's Book of Farm Management and Country Life: a complete cyclopaedia of rural occupations.* Wood & Lock Company Ltd., London.

Watt, K. Jane. 2000. Milk Stories. *A history of the Dairy Industry in British Columbia, 1827-2000.* Dairy Industry Historical Society of British Columbia.

Whetham, E.H. 1964. *The London Milk Trade, 1860-1900. The Economic History Review*, New Series, 17 (2), 369-380.

A classification for collectors of milk cans and containers in the image of a milk can.

The word 'can' is used in a generic sense because not all milk cans were or are made of metal. The term 'milk' is used in a generic sense and could include 'cream'. I define 'milk can' as a container (usually with a lid) commonly made of metal and used for carrying or transporting milk or cream (from cows, buffalos and other domestic animals). This includes small hand-held containers (up to about two pints) once commonly used by members of the household. It does not include milk jugs or milk bottles.

Category 1. Real milk cans.

(Either) cans that have been designed and constructed for the function of transporting or carrying milk (or)

Cans that were functional milk cans but are now no longer suitable for that purpose and in some cases have been painted for garden ornaments or modified for another purpose (e.g. light stand, garden roller, or lemonade dispenser). No matter what function they now serve, if any, they were originally real milk cans.

Category 2.

Replica 'cans' made in the image and size of real milk cans.

These are 'decorative' containers and are not designed to contain anything in particular.

Category 3.

Containers made in the image of milk cans.

These have the shape of the 'traditional' milk can but have another function such as a light shade or a container (e.g. for chocolates, glue, condiments, biscuits).

Category 4.

Toy and miniature milk cans. These are either toy milk cans or miniature ornamental milk cans such as found on charm bracelets.

EPILOGUE

In August 1913, the following commentary appeared in several English Newspapers.

Milk Can Doomed.

Important Decision of London Dairies.

The doom of the milk can has been decreed. Within a brief time, it is hoped, milk will no longer be ladled out in dusty streets, catching the germs that hover around.

It will be delivered in all cases in sealed bottles which will be filled in the dairy. In addition, no milk older than thirty-six hours will be served to the public. These decisions have been reached at a conference in London attended by a number of the largest dairy firms.

It was unanimously resolved at the conference that the time had arrived when voluntary milk certification, which has been urged by farmers, dairymen, and consumers alike, should be based on the rules and regulations relating to the sale of milk observed by the Department of Health in the City of New York. The chief of these regulations are as follows:

Milk shall be delivered to the consumer only in sealed bottles, which have been sealed at the dairy.

Milk shall be delivered to the consumer within thirty-six hours from the time at which it was drawn.

Regarding milk for cooking and manufacturing purposes only, the requirements are that the caps of all the bottles shall be of a certain colour and design, and shall have the words "for cooking only" affixed. Milk under the designation of "condensed" or "concentrated" shall only be sold under a special permit.

Among the sanitary requirements there is an important provision:-

"Every wholesale dealer shall keep a record in his office to show the place from which milk or cream was delivered by him daily to retail stores has been received; and the said record shall be kept for a period of two months for inspection by the Department of Health, and shall be readily accessible to the inspectors of the said department".

Fourteen years later, there was equally widely distributed news headed with "Eclipse of the Milk Can". A photograph said it all: A glass lined railway milk tank which carries 3,000 gallons or quantity equal to the capacity of the 300 empty milk churns standing on the railway platform.

CREDITS

▲ *A Sexton (U.S.A.) wall plaque dated 1975. No. 59964.*
This image is used at the start of each section in part one.

Images shown at the start of each section in part two.

HISTORY AND DESIGN.

A souvenir platter from the Dresden Dairy, Germany. Established in 1880 the Dairy has become known the world over for its beautiful hand-painted tiles. This scene shows two cherubs and a milk cart filled with small milk cans pulled by dog.

PROMOTING AND ADVERTISING MILK CANS.

Cohen's Full Cream Dairy van (Victoria, Birmingham, 1920) with the cab shaped like a milk churn. A Chronicle/Alamy Stock Photo. Image G3AWM3.

PATENTS FOR MILK CANS.

U.S.A Patent No. 315,371. 1885. A milk can or carrier patented by R.B. Anderson.

ACCESSORIES.

A 1930 advertisement for the Cream City Giant Sanitary Milk Filtering Strainer.

PROCESSING AND MAINTENANCE.

'A travelling tinker' circa 1900. Courtesy of Palmerston North Libraries and Community Services.

THE DAIRY FARM AND SOCIAL ASPECTS

This photograph postcard dates from 1940 during the severe winter of 1939-40 in Britain. On the back of the card it says "Haslingden New Road, the only way to carry milk through the drifts".

TRANSPORT.

A miniature milk moneybox can on a four-wheeled trolley.

UPCYCLING – A NEW LEASE OF LIFE.

The remains of a garden roller made out of three cylindrical milk cans, each about 20 inches (50 cm.) long and filled with concrete.

MILK CAN ART.

Courtesy of Shem Sutherland from Dunedin, New Zealand.

MILK CANS AND THE ARTS.

Part of a post card painting by T. Grilson, well known for his art during the First World War.

IN THE IMAGE OF THE MILK CAN.

A particularly innovative milk can design for a mobile services trailer by ROKA Werk GembH, based in Mengerskirchen. Germany.

MINIATURES AND TOY MILK CANS.

A model or ornament (Copyright E.B.L.) of Enid Blyton's 'Noddy' with a milk perambulator, milk bottle crate and a milk can.

MILK CAN GAMES, SPORTS AND ENTERTAINMENT.

An illustration showing the basics of a fairground game called 'milk can'.

NOSTALGIA.

Milk Churn Planters made by Narrowboat & Canal Ware http://www.blackcountrymetalworks.co.uk/milk-churn-planters.htm

MODERN MILK CANS.

Plastic milk cans. Ashish Cans & Containers PVT LTD., pioneers in manufacturing plastic milk cans in India.

CONVERSION FACTORS (LB = POUND WEIGHT)

1 pint = 568 cc.

1 Imperial gallon = 8 pints = 1.2 U.S. gallons = 4.54 litres.

1 U.S. gallon = 0.83 Imperial gallon = 3.77 litres.

1 litre = 1.76 pints = 0.22 Imperial gallon = 0.264 U.S. gallons

6 U.S. gallons = 5 Imperial gallons approx.

1 pint of milk weighs 20.64 oz = 585 grams.

1 Imperial gallon of milk weighs 10.32 lb = 3.90 kg.

1 U.S. gallon of milk = 8.6 lb = 3.90 kg.

1 Imperial gallon of water weighs 10 lb = 4.54 kg.

THE JOURNEY IS
AT AN END

ABOUT THE AUTHOR

Ian Spellerberg's interest in milk cans commenced when he was a boy on his uncle's farm. He has fond memories of milking time and the milk cans. Years later he found that very little had been written about milk cans and subsequently he started to assemble a collection of cans from around the world. They are now found both inside and outside his home in New Zealand. They fill outbuildings and welcome you at the gate. Ian's book is a celebration of the milk can. He fevently hopes that the iconic milk can will find a place in a museum of art and design.

Ian is an established author with many articles published about antiques and collectibles. He has also published two books: *Match Holders: first-hand accounts of tinerboxes, matches, spills, vesta cases, match strikers, and permanent matches* and *Reading & Writing Accessories: a study of paper knives, paper folders, letter openers, and mythical page turners.*